BRAVER TOGETHER

Braver Together

VOL.1

Amy Tarpein

Mug Memoirs Publishing

Dedication

To my incredible mini humans, who have shown me more about life and how to truly live it than I ever imagined. Being your momma has been an absolute gift.

To Mike, thank you for being my biggest encourager and for believing in me every step of the way. Whether it was showing up with coffee when I needed it most or reminding me why I started, I will always remember the Packers table...

To my Zoom ladies, a divine selection of women who embody Christ's love with their warm hugs and invaluable advice. Your constant, prayers, presence, and unwavering support mean the world to me.
To my sister's blood and chosen, thank you for always reminding me who I am!

To all of you scattered across the globe, too many to name individually here
who pray for us, encourage us, and love us my love for you runs deep.
To the countless souls who have shown me the true meaning of courage and unity.

To my readers, thank you for embarking on this journey with me. Your support and shared experiences are the heartbeat of this book.

May we all continue to be braver together, facing life's challenges with love, strength, and unwavering faith.

Contents

Foreword

Amy's narrative as a single mother of ten, with her youngest son diagnosed with Lissencephaly, complex issues, and a terminal prognosis, epitomizes bravery and resilience. In her book "Braver Together," she candidly recounts her real-life journey, navigating through challenges and joys while embarking on global adventures with her five younger children to create lasting memories and share their stories with the world. With unwavering faith and the steadfast support of her "mini-humans" and her community, her story magnificently illustrates the strength of community and the potency of faith. Though life presents obstacles, with the right allies, a sprinkle of faith, and "copious amounts of coffee" overcoming them is possible. Embark on Amy's touching voyage of hope and determination, a truly uplifting narrative for everyone. Keep those tissues close; this heartfelt book is sure to touch your soul.

Amy's account serves as a poignant reminder of the significance of a robust support network and the resilience innate in the human spirit. Through her tales of hardship and victories, readers will be deeply moved by the love and commitment of Amy and her family, along with the unyielding faith that sees her through the toughest moments. "Braver Together" is a must-read for those seeking solace and motivation in the face of adversity. Amy's book is not just a testament to her personal strength, but also a beacon of hope for others facing similar challenges. Each chapter offers a glimpse into the heart of a mother who refuses to let life's difficulties dim her spirit. The vivid descriptions of her family's travels, from bustling cityscapes to serene countryside retreats, paint a picture of a life lived fully despite the shadows of illness and hardship.

Readers will find themselves captivated by the intimate and honest portrayals of Amy's day-to-day life. Her anecdotes range from the humorous mishaps of traveling with a large family to the tender, quiet moments of connection that illuminate the profound bonds between her and her children. These stories are interwoven with reflections on the power of community, the importance of cherishing every moment, and the incredible strength that can be found in vulnerability.

"Braver Together" also serves as a call to action, encouraging readers to build and nurture their own support networks. Amy's experiences highlight how essential it is to lean on friends, family, and even strangers in times of need. Her journey underscores the message that no one is truly alone, and that help and kindness can be found in the most unexpected places.

Ultimately, Amy's story is one of triumph. It is a reminder that even in the face of seemingly insurmountable odds, love and faith can light the way forward. Her unwavering positivity and relentless pursuit of joy are inspirational, offering a roadmap for others to follow when the path seems dark and uncertain.

"Braver Together" is more than just a memoir; it is a celebration of life, love, and the indomitable human spirit. It is a book that will not only resonate with those who have faced similar struggles but will also inspire anyone who believes in the power of perseverance and the extraordinary resilience of the human heart.

A Note From The Author

Wherever two or more gather in my name, I will be there.

    This book is a guiding light, reminding you that you are cherished and never on your own. It serves as a beacon, guiding you on your journey ahead. Through its pages, I aim to impart wisdom to you, my children, and future generations, even in my absence. Certain challenges in life cannot be fixed only carried. I hold the belief that God sends people to help us bear these burdens, for we are Braver Together.

Dear reader,

Welcome! If we haven't met before, I hope that you will consider me a friend by the end of this book. And if we have already crossed paths, welcome back! It's an honor to be in your company! Regardless of our previous acquaintance, I hope that you will find this experience as enriching as I did while living and writing it.

These journal entries began as a daily record of my attempts to live through the challenging life I found myself in. This isn't the life I had envisioned for myself, but looking back, I can see that I was never alone, and neither are you.

Throughout these pages, you will walk with me through moments of joy and sorrow, triumph and defeat, love and loss. Each entry is a snapshot of a day in my life, a piece of the intricate mosaic that forms my journey. As you read, I encourage you to reflect on your own path, to see the strength and resilience within yourself, and to know that every step you take is a part of your unique story.

You will find tales of friendships that shaped me, challenges that tested me, and dreams that fueled my spirit. Some days were filled with laughter, others with tears, but each was a lesson in its own right. I hope that my experiences will resonate with you, reminding you that even in our darkest hours, there is always a glimmer of light.

So, let us embark on this journey together. Turn the page, and let the stories unfold. May you find comfort, inspiration, and perhaps even a bit of yourself in these words. Thank you for joining me on this journey.

Amy

The Backstory

Let's Begin with the Background.

When interacting with readers, one of the most common inquiries I receive pertains to the backstory of my life and Elijah's Baby Bucket List. How do I manage being a single parent? And what drives me to continue pushing forward? The short answer is Jesus, copious amounts of coffee, and the combined strength of the people who walk through this with us.

Over time, I have realized that an individual's backstory is the most intriguing aspect. It is where you uncover the lessons and magic intertwined within their journey.

What truly amazes me are the divine interventions that led me to my current position. The unexpected encounters that brought this book to fruition and now into your hands arose from all the prayers I believed went unheard.

I cannot adequately articulate the tears shed over what I once perceived as failures or setbacks: my abusive marriages, my mother's battle with cancer, my ex-husband's struggle with brain cancer and addiction, years of mistreatment, my divorce, and my son's terminal diagnosis.

These experiences have paved the way for the personal growth required to be where I am today.

They have taught me that some aspects of life cannot be fixed; they must simply be carried. There are people who come into our lives precisely when we need them. They sit by our side, at times with coffee and prayers in hand. It may be all they can offer, but facing challenges together somehow makes them more bearable because we are Braver Together!

Remember, you are not alone! Here are fragments of my life, shared in no particular sequence, that I hope can support you during challenging times.

My Life Is Not a Tragedy It Is a Testimony

Braver Together: A Journey of Joy, Resilience, and the Extraordinary

Braver Together: A Journey of Joy, Resilience, and the Extraordinary

Our story and this book are a testament to the boundless joy and resilience that can bloom even in the toughest of circumstances. Diagnosed with Lissencephaly, a rare and terminal condition, Elijah wasn't expected to live past the age of two. Yet, in a beautiful twist of fate, he celebrated his sixth birthday this past January. Elijah is a blessing! He is the embodiment of pure Joy and unconditional love! As our family embarks on a globe-trotting adventure to tick off his baby bucket list, we do so with a heart full of gratitude, choosing joy and living boldly every step of the way.

Now, let's address the elephant in the room: the book contains many references to God. For some readers, this might be a point of discomfort. But here's the thing—whether you share these beliefs or not, the core of Elijah's journey is something we can all relate to. It's about connection, encouragement, love, and support. Our diverse beliefs are what make our world so beautifully rich and textured. By keeping an open mind and continuing to read, you might find that we have more in common than you initially thought.

Through understanding and open-mindedness, we can build bridges where once there were walls. Let's embrace this journey with open hearts and minds, ready to learn from each other and grow together. It's about finding joy in the present and appreciating the beauty of life, even in the face of adversity. his book is more than just a narrative; it's an invitation to witness the extraordinary within the everyday, to see the light that shines even in the darkest of times. Elijah's story is a powerful reminder that life, in all its unpredictability, is still a precious gift. It urges us to cherish each moment, embrace our loved ones, and live with intention and courage.

As you turn each page, you'll not only follow our incredible journey but also reflect on your own. You'll see how challenges can be met with love, how laughter can be found in the simplest of moments, and how hope can persist against all odds. This isn't just a story about a boy with a rare condition; it's a universal tale about the human spirit's capacity for resilience and joy. So, dive in with a spirit of kindness and compassion, and let's discover the magic of living boldly and choosing joy together. We are Braver Together!

Every Superhero Has an Origin Story

LIVE LIFE SO COMPLETELY THAT WHEN DEATH COMES LIKE A THIEF IN THE NIGHT, THERE WILL BE NOTHING LEFT FOR IT TO TAKE

elijahslastbucketlist.com

Every superhero has an Origin story this is his!

Part one.

On August 22, 2018, my life took a sudden turn. This significant event is often referred to as D-day (diagnosis day). Not all disabilities are visible from the start. Some parents learn about their child's special needs before birth, while others discover them at birth or even years later. For me, it wasn't until eight months after Elijah was born that I first heard the term Lissencephaly. This marked the day when my son was diagnosed with this rare condition that impacts brain development. It is a genetic disorder that may not show immediate signs and can take time to identify. Hearing the diagnosis was a pivotal moment, forever altering our lives. The word "Lissencephaly" changed everything, creating a memory that will always stay with me.

Being a parent, accepting the diagnosis was a difficult process. Numerous questions and worries arose. How would this impact my child's future? What support would be necessary? How could I assist my child in achieving his best? These concerns consumed my thoughts at night. Despite the obstacles, I appreciate each day spent with my mini-humans. Elijah has taught us valuable lessons on love, faith, and the strength of the human soul. He has emphasized the significance of raising awareness about uncommon conditions such as Lissencephaly.

I sensed something was off from his MRI results and suspected he was experiencing seizures. I had the children with me, and just days before the appointment, he had started his first of several seizure medications. Uncertain about the news we might receive, we prepared to visit Aunt KK's.

Sitting in the neurologist's office, holding my sleeping baby boy while my other children waited in the waiting room, I felt a flood of emotions. Fear, anger, and devastation washed over me as the doctor told me "Elijah's diagnosis is terminal." I absorbed the news of his "limitations" and prognosis. The doctor's somber list of what Elijah would never accomplish was truly heartbreaking.

I had to ask him to spell out his condition twice as it was unfamiliar to me. He mentioned that Elijah would not survive beyond the age of two. Elijah would require a feeding tube, be in a vegetative state, unable to walk, and may not ever recognize us. Developmentally, he would not progress beyond 2-3 months. He has since surpassed all those expectations!

I felt a compelling urge to shout expletives at the universe! It was like a burning coal lodged in my chest. Despite trying to suppress it, the feeling lingered. I was frozen with fear. "Can I handle this? No, I can't. Yes, I must." Taking a deep breath, I prayed fervently. I began envisioning ways to support him in his success. At that moment, as I sat there with the Doctor I said "If he only has two years, I want to make sure they are the most fulfilling and God-filled years possible."

I left that office and entered a world that was forever altered. As I walked through the lobby I had to consciously remind myself to breathe: Inhale, exhale, repeat. Gathering my children and my emotions, we found our way to our car. I struggled to contain my fears, anger, and sorrow, shielding them from view. It was crucial for me to remain steadfast, a symbol of hope, and a pillar of strength as we navigate this unfamiliar and daunting journey.

As I tried to embrace the reality of Elijah's diagnosis, I found myself navigating a whirlwind of emotions and uncertainties. The weight of the neurologist's words echoed in my mind, painting a picture of the challenges that lay ahead. Yet, amidst the fear and despair, I clung to a glimmer of hope and determination. Holding my sleeping baby in my arms, I made a silent vow to make every moment count — to fill his days with love, joy, and unwavering faith. I resolved that if his life was to be brief, we would provide him with the most enriching life possible.

The path ahead appeared challenging, filled with unknowns and barriers. However, as a parent, I understood the need to stay strong for my children, shielding them from the emotional turmoil within me. In moments of quiet contemplation in the children's hospital parking lot with my six kids. I gathered my resolve and prepared to confront the obstacles ahead. My life took a new direction. Our plans changed.

Originally intending to visit my sister in Texas, The sorrow weighed heavily in my throat like a burning ember. Despite swallowing hard, the grief persisted. I made a decision to head to the ocean, a promise made long ago after my divorce but never fulfilled. Given two years, what could I do? I desired more than just the Gulf, so I looked up Florida Beaches. Among my top results was Jacksonville Beach. After researching the distance to the ocean, we altered our plans and I opted to embark on a 13-hour drive to Jacksonville, Florida, through the mountains with six kids.

Each breath became a reminder of resilience, each exhale a release of pent-up emotions. I knew the journey ahead would be tough, but I was determined to be a beacon of hope for my family. As we embarked on this new chapter filled with unknowns, I clung to the belief that love, faith, and unwavering determination would light our path through the darkness. And with each step forward, I vowed to make Elijah's journey one filled with God's boundless love, unwavering support, and endless possibilities. And soften the blow of the news I was going to have to give my mini-humans.

So I started driving. With each mile that passed on our journey to Jacksonville, Florida, the weight of the unknown future lifted slightly from my shoulders. The children chattered excitedly in the backseat, their innocent laughter a balm to my weary soul. The road stretched out before us, winding through the mountains, a metaphor for the twists and turns of life that lay ahead.

As the sun dipped below the horizon and the stars began to twinkle in the night sky, I found solace in the simple beauty of the moment. Elijah, nestled in his car seat, slept soundly, his tiny breaths a reminder of the fragile gift of life. I whispered silent prayers for strength and guidance, vowing to make every moment count and to fill Elijah's days with laughter and love, regardless of the challenges we faced. I drove until I couldn't stay awake.

Our first stop was a small hotel in the mountains. I settled the kids in bed and as soon as I knew they were asleep I held him close and sobbed I don't think I could have held him any closer! My heart ached. This was the scariest thing I had ever faced and I was facing it alone. Or so I thought! As I cried myself to sleep listening to him breathe and smelling his baby fresh smell. I prayed. I prayed from the bottom of my soul and I sobbed and bargained, I prayed some more.

As the night deepened, and the world outside fell into a hushed stillness, I felt a sense of peace settle over me, despite the weight of uncertainty that lingered. The hotel room was a temporary sanctuary, a haven amidst the storm of emotions raging within me. In the quiet darkness, I found myself reflecting on the journey that had brought us here, on the strength that had carried us through every trial and tribulation.

With Elijah nestled in my arms, his innocent face relaxed in slumber, I made a silent promise to him and to myself – to face each new day with courage, to embrace the challenges that lay ahead with unwavering determination. The road to Jacksonville was just the beginning of a new chapter, a chapter filled with unknown adventures and unexpected blessings.

Elijah's origin story part two.
Cades Cove

As the first light of dawn crept through the curtains, casting a soft glow over the room, I knew that no matter what obstacles awaited us, we would face them together, bound by a love that transcended fear and doubt. And so, as the world outside stirred to life once more, I whispered a prayer of gratitude for the strength that had brought us this far and the hope that would carry us through whatever lay ahead.

During a visit to a local salon for Isaiah's haircut, my interest in Tennessee prompted me to ask the stylist for recommendations. Enthusiastically, she suggested "Cades Cove," a charming free attraction. A quick online search revealed it was just a four-hour drive away. I live in Illinois that's a day trip.

As we journeyed through the mountains, we couldn't resist stopping for picturesque moments. The stunning beauty of the place left me speechless.

I often feel as if I am receiving unexpected lessons in grace and patience from a higher power when I am driving with my kids. In this case, three of the kids got voice-changing megaphones in their Happy Meals. Have you really learned patience if you haven't driven through the mountains with three kids, repeatedly chanting, "Are we there yet?" into the aforementioned megaphones? One can't help but think that God has a sense of humor!

We arrived just in time to enjoy a picnic dinner at the park entrance, where we chatted with the rangers to learn more about the history and received advice on avoiding contact with wildlife.

As we savored our picnic dinner at the park entrance, surrounded by the serene beauty of Cades Cove, I couldn't help but marvel at the wonders of nature that unfolded before us. The majestic mountains stood tall and proud, their peaks reaching for the heavens, while the lush greenery danced in the gentle breeze, whispering tales of ancient secrets.

Isaiah's eyes sparkled with excitement as he scanned the horizon, hoping to catch a glimpse of a bear, his adventurous spirit eager for a wild encounter. Meanwhile, Elijah's laughter filled the air, a joyful melody that echoed through the valley, a reminder of the pure innocence that graced our lives.

As we ventured further into the heart of the cove, following the winding paths that led us deeper into the wilderness, I felt a sense of peace settle over me, a tranquility that transcended the chaos of the world outside.

In that moment, surrounded by my mini humans and the untamed beauty of Cades Cove, I felt a deep sense of gratitude wash over me. Gratitude for the journey that had brought us here, for the challenges that had shaped us, and for the love that bound us together as a family. As we made our way back to the car, I knew that no matter where the road may lead us next, we would always have each other, our hearts intertwined in a bond that could weather any storm.

While leaving Cades Cove, we discovered that the GPS was not functioning. Opting to follow the road, we planned to stay wherever a hotel was found. Eventually, we arrived at Pigeon Forge, where we stumbled upon a wonderful hotel with a water park. I held Elijah while the kids played and had the pool all to themselves.

Afterward, we went inside and witnessed the sunset from our balcony. The sun dipped below the horizon, casting the sky in shades of pink and orange, showcasing nature's beauty. Above us, the stars sparkled like guiding lights.

As the night progressed, we prepared our food in our room and enjoyed a cozy family dinner together. The children were full of excitement, recounting their favorite moments from the day while Elijah peacefully napped in my arms.

After dinner, we took a stroll around the hotel grounds, marveling at the serene surroundings and crisp night air. The sound of laughter and joy filled the air as families gathered around, creating a warm and welcoming atmosphere.

Back in our room, I tucked the kids into bed, their faces filled with contentment and dreams of the adventures that awaited us the next day. As I sat alone on the balcony, I gazed out at the moon, which cast a soft glow over the landscape, adding a touch of magic to the night illuminating our path forward. The cool evening breeze whispered through the trees, carrying with it the comforting scent of pine.

As I sat there I prayed reflected on the day's adventures and felt grateful for the moments we shared. Amidst heartache, it's natural to feel anxious and worried. I shed countless tears, questioning why so much pain had to occur. Doubts surfaced about trusting again, fearing my heart would be broken once more after enduring so much over the past 8 years. In these fearful thoughts, I heard a question: "Do you have faith in my plan or not?" At the core, it all comes down to faith – the belief that life will unfold as intended, even if it leads to challenging and painful situations. I wholeheartedly believe that there is a plan in place, as I have witnessed its evidence too many times to ignore. This means holding onto that belief, even when the journey is complex, difficult, or uncertain.

Reflecting back, I see instances in my life where I was upset for not receiving something, only to realize later that it was never meant for me. Now, considering my current circumstances, I understand that our time with our children is temporary. It's about making the most of the time we have. We all play a role in each other's journeys, serving as guides and shaping one another as we move closer to our spiritual destinations.

Embracing the truth of the present situation strengthens my bond with God. Despite losing external sources of joy, having God by my side ensures my mental and emotional well-being. It's essential to remember that God's timing is perfect, and not being where you expected to be may lead you to exactly where you are meant to be.

In that peaceful moment, surrounded by my mini humans and the beauty of the natural world, I knew that this spontaneous journey had led us to a place of pure serenity. And as the night deepened, enveloping us in its gentle embrace, I drifted off to sleep feeling truly blessed.

Part three of Elijah's origin story.
Blood Mountain

The following morning, we departed from our hotel and set off for Blood Mountain, the highest point on the Appalachian Trail. As we traversed up the rugged terrain of Blood Mountain, the crisp mountain air filled our lungs, invigorating us for the challenging trek ahead. The sunlight filtered through the canopy of leaves, casting a warm glow on the forest floor. Each step brought us closer to the summit, where a breathtaking view awaited us.

Reaching the top of Blood Mountain, we sat and took in the panoramic vista of rolling hills and distant peaks. It was a moment of serenity and triumph, a reminder of the beauty and resilience of nature. We sat for a while, absorbing the tranquility of the mountains before descending back down the trail.

As we trekked back to the car from Blood Mountain, our hearts were still filled with the sense of accomplishment and wonder from reaching its summit. The memories of the breathtaking views and the peaceful moments spent at the top lingered in our minds as we made our way to Jacksonville.

Reflecting on our journey, I couldn't help but appreciate the strong sense of camaraderie among fellow hikers we had encountered along the trail. The shared experiences, the encouraging words, and the mutual respect for nature created a bond that transcended individual differences.

As we headed towards Jacksonville, the anticipation of future adventures stirred within us. The unknown trails and uncharted territories called out to our adventurous spirits, igniting a sense of excitement for what lay beyond the horizon.

Our journey to Blood Mountain not only tested our physical endurance but also enriched our souls with the beauty of nature and the warmth of human connection. Leaving Elijah's shoes behind was a symbolic gesture, a tribute to the countless stories woven into the fabric of the trail by those who had walked its paths before us and alongside us!

As we drove away, the memories of our time on the trail lingered like a sweet melody, inspiring us to seek out more moments of tranquility, triumph, and togetherness in the great adventure that is life. Our hearts were filled with gratitude for the experience and our minds were already dreaming of the next adventure that awaited us, ready to embrace the unknown with open arms. As we sat together to recount our adventures, we knew that this was just the beginning of many more journeys to come.

Leaving behind Elijah's shoes as a token of our journey was a poignant gesture, a way to connect with the countless other hikers who had passed through these woods. As we continued on our path toward Jacksonville, we carried with us the memories of our adventure, the camaraderie of the trail, and the spirit of exploration that bound us together. Our hearts were full, our spirits lifted, and our minds already wandering to the next adventure that awaited us beyond the horizon.

Part four of Elijah's origin story.
Jacksonville Beach Florida.

Upon our arrival in Jacksonville, we were welcomed by the salty ocean breeze, bringing a feeling of tranquility and new beginnings. Witnessing their eyes widen in amazement at the expansive sea, Elijah's laughter echoed with the crashing waves. Surrounded by my mini humans and the endless horizon, I realized that our journey was just starting. As we sat there, gazing at the ocean together for the first time, I shared Elijah's diagnosis with them – that he wouldn't have a long life. Despite this, we made a promise to give him the best life possible.

Isaiah protested, "That's unfair!" I prepared to explain that some things cannot be fixed. Then he quipped, "Elijah gets to go to heaven without being good!" We all chuckled. Life isn't always fair, is it?

My children were baptized in the ocean, marking the inception of Elijah's Baby Bucket List to show him all the wonders he should experience before he goes.

As the sun dipped below the horizon, casting a warm golden glow over the water, we set out on a mission to fulfill Elijah's Baby Bucket List. From building sandcastles on the shore to chasing seagulls along the pier, each moment was a precious memory etched in our hearts. We explored the vibrant marine life, marveled at the towering lighthouse, and indulged in sweet treats at the local ice cream parlor.

The days have turned into weeks, and weeks have turned into years, and our adventures have taken us beyond the sandy beaches of Jacksonville. We have ventured into the lush forests, climbed majestic mountains, and sailed across crystal-clear lakes. Elijah's eyes sparkle with joy as he experiences the wonders of the world, his laughter a melody that fills our souls with love and gratitude.

Through it all, we hold each other close, embracing the beauty of the present moment and cherishing the time we have together. As the waves whispered tales of resilience and hope, we know that Elijah's spirit holds that same resilience.

And so, under the vast expanse of the universe, we vowed to continue our journey with courage and grace, guided by the light of Elijah's unwavering love and joy. For in his laughter, in his innocence, we found the true meaning of life – to live fully, to love deeply, and to cherish every precious moment we are given.

As we build Elijah's baby bucket list and document his adventures, I am filled with gratitude for the unexpected blessings that have come our way. Each day with Elijah is a gift a reminder to embrace the present moment and cherish the ones we love.

Through our story, we hope to inspire others to find strength in their faith, to hold onto hope in the face of adversity, and to never underestimate the power of love in transforming lives.

We dream of starting a nonprofit to support families like ours, I am filled with a sense of purpose and determination. Our journey may be filled with challenges, but with love as our compass, faith as our guide, and copious amounts of coffee, I am confident that we can weather any storm that comes our way. Elijah's light shines bright, illuminating the path ahead with endless possibilities and boundless love.

Living With Open Hands

Living with open hands and accepting life's twists is important.

The year 2023 has taught me to welcome life with open hands. Often, we have a preferred story about how our lives should have turned out. It's easy to become fixated on our plans and expectations, but reality doesn't always align with our visions. My personal story is no exception. However, I've realized I would not have had the courage to write my story as God has written it, with all its twists and turns. This is why I choose to rely on His guidance and live with open hands.

Elijah's story is a powerful example of living with open hands. Despite his terminal diagnosis, we chose to embrace each moment with joy and gratitude, completing his bucket list and exploring the world together. Our story reminds you that life is a precious gift, and we should make the most of every moment.

In retrospect, I can see the goodness of God, even when things don't go according to my plan. It's important to remember that God is still God, no matter what happens.

Living with open hands requires courage and vulnerability. It can be scary to let go of our plans and expectations, especially when we don't know what the future holds. However, by embracing the unknown and being willing to take risks, we can discover new passions and purpose.

This is a powerful reminder that life is a precious gift, and we should accept it with open hands. When we grip our plans and expectations too tightly, we risk overlooking the unexpected blessings that come our way. By trusting in God's guidance and living with open hands, we can fully embrace all life offers.

As we move forward, let us remember that each day is a new opportunity to practice living with open hands. This mindset allows us to be more present, more adaptive, and more grateful for the small moments that make life beautiful. Whether it's a simple act of kindness from a stranger, an unexpected opportunity, or a challenge that pushes us to grow, every experience contributes to the richness of our lives.

Living with open hands doesn't mean we relinquish all control or ambition. Instead, it means we hold our dreams and goals lightly, allowing room for divine intervention and the unexpected paths that can lead to growth and fulfillment. It's about balancing our aspirations with a humble acceptance that we don't have all the answers, and that sometimes, the best outcomes arise from the most unplanned circumstances.

As we continue this journey, let us support one another in our efforts to live with open hands. Share your stories, your struggles, and your triumphs. Encourage those around you to embrace the unpredictability of life with grace and courage. Together, we can create a community that thrives on trust, hope, and the unwavering belief that life, in all its complexity, is a gift to be cherished.

So, here's to living with open hands—embracing the unknown, celebrating the present, and trusting in the journey ahead. May we all find peace and joy in the beautiful tapestry of life that unfolds before us.

Discovering Faith Through Tragedy

Discovering Faith Through Tragedy:
A Mother's Lasting Gift of Belief

I once heard Dr. Chuck Sackett mention, "You can't really preach until you've buried your mother," and that resonated deep within me. In April 2010, I lost my mother to ovarian cancer, a time when I, formerly an atheist seeking answers, went through a profound trans-formation.

At the age of six, my infant sister passed away after just 28 days. This tragedy plunged my mother into a severe depression, where she spent her days sleeping and weeping on my grandmother's couch. Before this, we used to pray together every night. I vividly recall my 6-year-old self longing for those moments of prayer with her again. However, when I asked her if we could pray once more, she shattered my innocence by revealing that "God, Santa, and the Easter Bunny didn't exist. They were all made up."

This revelation sparked a lifelong quest for knowledge and under-standing. I immersed myself in various world religion courses during my college years, delved into the Bible, and devoured any religious texts within reach in search of meaning. In 2008, my mother was diagnosed with stage four ovarian cancer following a hysterectomy that inadver-tently damaged her spleen, leading to a delayed diagnosis.

On Easter Sunday, following an extensive surgery at 2 am, the surgeon, visibly exhausted, delivered grim news to my siblings and me in the waiting room. He somberly disclosed that my mother had a mere 4% chance of waking up, advising us to spend Easter with our family and be prepared for her imminent passing. He concluded by saying, "If you believe in God, you should pray."

Overwhelmed with emotion, I dropped to my knees in that waiting room, beseeching the God of my childhood to intervene. Miraculously, my mother awoke from her coma and lived for two more years. During this time, she had to relearn basic skills like telling time and driving, but most importantly, she gifted me with faith. Her first words upon awakening were a heartfelt admission, "I am SO sorry! I was wrong, and God is real!", having encountered God during her comatose state.

Every day until her passing, we conversed on the phone about God every morning over coffee and each evening, and she shared her new-found knowledge and faith gained during her time in that coma. She diligently emailed me scriptures daily. Her final words to me were re-assuring, "I am not going anywhere! I will always be there with you in spirit. Just talk to God like you talk to me! Hold tight to God, and God will send people!"

Her unwavering faith sustained me through my ex-husband's battle with brain cancer, my divorce, and the ongoing challenges I face today, instilling in me a deep faith and understanding of various religions. Though I lost my mother prematurely, she selflessly devoted the last years of her life to saving mine, leaving me eternally grateful for the invaluable lesson that God's goodness prevails even in life's storms.

Reflecting on Life's Magic

Adding Images to My Book and Reflecting on Life's Magic.

Currently, I'm formatting my book and adding pictures to it. I believe that God is an incredible artist and deserves to be celebrated. While I'm picking out which pictures to include, I can't help but feel emotional about how difficult, yet wondrous, my life has been.

Reflecting on my past experiences has helped me to recognize the magical moments that have shaped who I am today. From the challenges that have tested my resilience to the moments of joy that have filled my heart, all of it has contributed to my growth and development.

As I add these images to my book, I'm reminded of the people who have touched my life and the memories that we've shared. Each picture serves as a snapshot of a moment in time, frozen forever in my heart and mind.

It's amazing how a simple image can evoke so many emotions and memories. It's a powerful reminder to always cherish the moments that we have with the people who matter most to us.

As I continue with my book, I'm grateful for the opportunity to reflect on my life's journey and to celebrate all of the beauty and magic that it has held.

I hope that as you are reading this you will find inspiration in my story and see the beauty in your own life as well. Life is an intricate tapestry woven with threads of hardship and happiness, and each thread adds depth and richness to the overall picture.

As I turn each page, I am filled with a deep sense of gratitude for the experiences that have brought me to this moment. The laughter shared with friends, the tears shed in solitude, the victories won, and the lessons learned all form the essence of my journey.

In the end, this book is more than just a collection of words and images; it is a testament to the resilience of the human spirit and the profound beauty of our shared humanity. It is a celebration of life in all its forms, a reminder that even in the darkest times, there is light to be found.

I hope that through my story, you will find the courage to embrace your journeys with an open heart and to see the extraordinary in the ordinary. For it is in these moments, both big and small, that the true magic of life is revealed.

Some Things in Life Cannot be Fixed

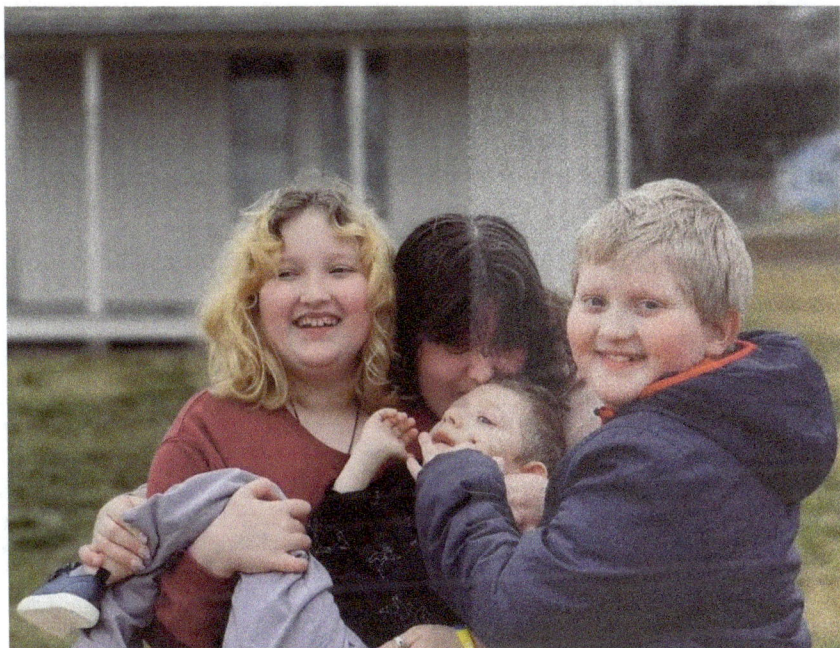

Some things in life cannot be fixed; they can only be carried.

Life is full of challenges that cannot always be fixed, no matter how well-intentioned we are. Broken hearts, mistakes that have altered the course of a life, and terminal diagnoses are just a few examples. However, by walking alongside those who are struggling and sharing our light, we have the ability to make a difference. Even in the face of reason, we can bring hope and positivity to those in need.

While there are many things we cannot control, let us focus on what we can do daily to make a positive impact. Some things in life cannot be fixed; they can only be carried, and I believe God sends people to help us carry them because we are braver together!

I am so thankful for the Divinely directed detours and people who led me to God. I can do hard things because I have a community that helps light my path. We can't fix the big things in life or our past mistakes. But we can face whatever comes our way together with Love.

Love has an incredible way of transforming our burdens into bearable loads. It's in the small acts of kindness, the gentle words of encouragement, and the silent presence of a friend that we find the strength to carry on. Each of us has the power to be a beacon of light, guiding others through their darkest moments.

As we journey through this life, let us remember to extend grace not only to others but also to ourselves. Forgiveness, both given and received, can lighten the heaviest of loads. Embrace the imperfections and acknowledge that our worth is not determined by our ability to fix everything but by our capacity to love and support one another.

In the end, it's the connections we build, the love we share, and the compassion we show that truly define us.

Kaleidoscope

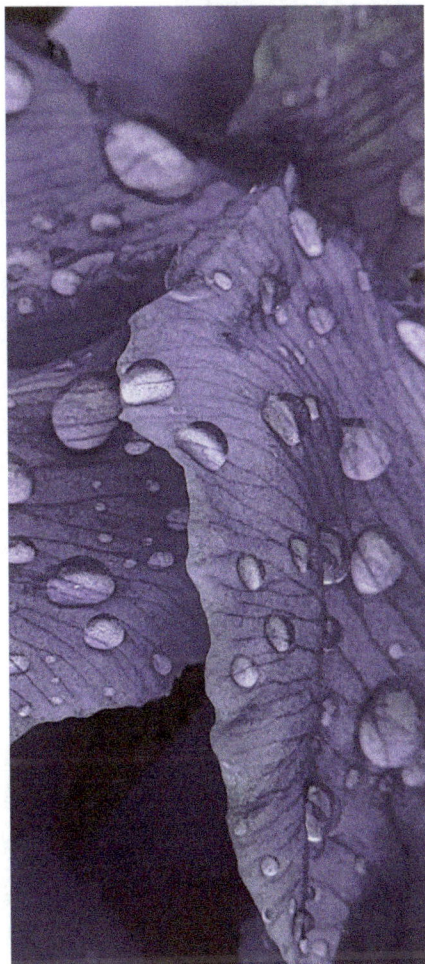

Kaleidoscope

I have spent fourteen years working at the Post Office. It was a typical Saturday, I was supposed to be working, but then I got distracted thinking about life and kaleidoscopes! The weather was so dull and rainy, and I was feeling blah. But guess what? I found so much beauty in the middle of the storm!

The last few weeks have been so crazy for me. I have been solo parenting my five kids, and one of them has special needs. Let me tell you, it's not easy on the best days. On the worst days, it feels like I am trying to get through that spinning kaleidoscope tube in a funhouse! When the worst days are strung together into a week or even a few weeks, solo parenting becomes an exercise in simply trying not to fall off the ride.

But then I get to work, and surprisingly enough, I get to slow down. I listen to my bible app and spend some much-needed time alone with God and my thoughts. And when things have slowed down, I am reminded of something important. We don't seek life's storms, but they will come. And we can find beauty in them.

Sometimes, beauty is more potent in the middle of the storm. Today, I am reminded of just how much beauty I have in my life! Have you heard of the verse in Ecclesiastes 3:11 that says, "He has made everything beautiful in its time. He has also set eternity in the human heart, yet no one can fathom what God has done from beginning to end"? It's so true!

Reflecting on this verse gives me a sense of peace and a deeper understanding of the journey I'm on. It's not always easy to see the beauty when you're caught in the whirlwind of life's challenges, but when I pause and look around, I realize that beauty is woven through even the most chaotic moments. My children's laughter, the way the rain sounds against the window, and the brief, quiet moments of solitude—all these are reminders of the beauty that exists amidst the storm.

Life is a series of seasons, each with its unique challenges and blessings. As I navigate through my own, I hold onto the belief that there is a greater purpose to every trial and triumph. This perspective helps me to embrace each day with gratitude and hope, knowing that even the hardest days contribute to the beautiful tapestry of my life.

I've come to see my time at the Post Office as more than just a job; it's a sanctuary where I can find moments of reflection and clarity. It's in these quiet times that I feel most connected to God and the deeper meaning of my experiences. I am reminded that, like a kaleidoscope, every turn and shift in my life creates a new and intricate pattern, each one more beautiful than the last.

So, as I move forward, I choose to focus on the beauty amid the storm. I choose to see the kaleidoscope of my life not as a chaotic jumble, but as a dynamic and ever-changing masterpiece. And in doing so, I find strength, peace, and a renewed sense of purpose.

My Life is Not a Tragedy

My life is not a tragedy.

Some things in life can't be fixed, only carried! I am so thankful for the Divinely directed detours and people who led me to God. I can do hard things because.

" The Lord is my shepherd; I shall not want. He maketh me to lie down in green pastures: he leadeth me beside the still waters. He restoreth my soul: he leadeth me in the paths of righteousness for his name's sake. Yea, though I walk through the valley of the shadow of death, I will fear no evil: for thou art with me; thy rod and thy staff they comfort me. Thou preparest a table before me in the presence of mine enemies: thou anointest my head with oil; my cup runneth over. Surely goodness and mercy shall follow me all the days of my life: and I will dwell in the house of the Lord forever. "

I am a solo mom and believe it or not, life is not always chaotic. A couple of hours, as the sun rises, it is calm. Before the kids are awake, and the crazy kicks in. It's just me, Jesus, and coffee! The house is quiet, and I can kneel humbly and intentionally take on whatever the day has in store.

He leads me. He comforts me. My cup overflows with blessings and gratitude, not just my coffee cup. I know that He sends people. When I don't know how I am going to take one more seemingly catastrophic event, I am reminded that I can do hard things because I am not alone in my struggles. We are made to connect with people. Sometimes, the only thing I can do is hold on to God and pray. But I am never praying alone! That is my greatest secret, the source of my unwavering faith and hope!

My life is a hot mess, but I'm His hot mess. I could break down and lament, and sometimes I do! But I keep getting up. In the face of fear and uncertainty, I have decided that I will keep moving forward. Towards a future, I might need more imagination to see. Because His way, while MUCH more complex than I would have chosen, has changed my life and given me a gift and understanding, I don't think I could have found my way.

I know deep in my soul I won't waste all the lessons I learn. I pray that all of my life, especially the hot mess, is a testimony of what God can do in the human heart! This morning, I am reminded that my life is not a tragedy. It is a testimony!

I choose to embrace each moment, each challenge, and each blessing with the knowledge that I am guided by a higher purpose. My journey, though filled with twists and turns, is a testament to resilience and faith. I find comfort in the quiet mornings, as they are a sacred time of renewal and reflection, a space where I can gather my strength and remember the profound love and support that surrounds me.

In those still moments, I am reminded of the beauty in the chaos. My children's laughter, the small victories, and even the tears. I am learning to see the divine in every day, to find grace in imperfection, and to trust that each step I take is part of a greater plan.

As I navigate through my day, I carry with me the words of Psalm 23, a constant reminder of God's unwavering presence. I am never truly alone, for His guidance and love are my companions. And with each obstacle I overcome, I grow stronger, more compassionate, and more attuned to the miracles that unfold around me.

So, I move forward with a heart full of gratitude and a spirit ready to embrace whatever comes my way. I am not defined by the messiness of my life, but by the faith and determination that drive me. My story is one of hope and transformation, a living testament to the power of divine love and the strength found in community and connection.

Today, I choose to live out my testimony with joy and courage, knowing that even in the midst of uncertainty, I am held by a love that never fails. And that, to me, is the greatest gift of all.

Learn to Appreciate the Beauty

Learn to appreciate the beauty even during difficult times

Have you ever looked at a painting, listened to a symphony, or read a book and thought, "That's not how I would have done it"? Or have you been upset with how a story went? Maybe they killed off your favorite character, or the plot took a turn you didn't expect. I wonder if this is how our Creator must feel as he watches our lives unfold.

When Vincent van Gogh painted The Starry Night, he had no idea how significant it would become. The painting depicts the view from the east-facing window of his asylum room just before sunrise, with the addition of an ideal village.

Right now, you may be at the soft part of your life's symphony, wondering and waiting for the crescendo. However, the Creator can see how amazing things will be if you simply "Don't Go Upstairs!" Sometimes, he sends people to help guide and direct you, to talk you out of going upstairs, or to remind you that no matter how bad things may seem, sometimes it's about being able to see The Starry Night while you're there.

He sends people to guide us, steer us in the right direction, or remind us that even in the darkest of times, there is a shining light. We can be that light for someone else, inspiring them to keep moving forward. So, let's be that guidepost and help others see the beauty in their lives.

Remember, every masterpiece, whether a painting, a piece of music, or a life story, is filled with moments of doubt and uncertainty. The brushstrokes of life can be chaotic and unpredictable, but it is precisely these moments that add depth and texture to our existence.

Just as Van Gogh's swirling night sky is composed of countless small strokes, our lives are made up of many small decisions and actions. Each one, no matter how insignificant it may seem at the time, contributes to the larger picture. Often, it is only when we step back and look at the whole canvas that we can truly appreciate the beauty of the design.

So, when you face those moments of frustration or confusion, remember that you are in the process of creating your masterpiece. Trust in the guidance you receive, whether it comes from within or from those around you. And have faith that, like The Starry Night, your life will one day be a source of inspiration for others.

As we continue on our journey, let's strive to be creators of light and hope. Let's offer a helping hand to those in need and be a beacon of encouragement for those who are struggling. By doing so, we not only enrich our own lives but also contribute to the beauty and harmony of the world around us.

In the grand symphony of life, each of us plays a vital part. Together, we can create a melody that resonates with love, compassion, and understanding, leaving a legacy that will be cherished for generations to come.

Fear Fades

Fear fades when we are brave together.

I recently went on a bucket list adventure to visit family for Easter and to help my baby Elijah tick off a few things from his bucket list. I witnessed my niece and daughter, who are only a few months apart in age, exploring a cave together that they were too scared to explore alone. They held hands and marched through the cold, knee-deep water like they were on a mission to conquer the world.

Their bravery led them to a stunning waterfall, which made me think of some of the relationships in my life. My sister came to mind first. She is currently facing one of the scariest times in her life as she tries to adopt two amazing little ones who have been through a lot in their short lives. Watching my sister's bravery and determination inspires me, especially as I deal with my baby's terminal diagnosis.

My sister charges forward with strength and courage, although fostering and adoption are never certain and can be challenging. She deals with triggers and tantrums while showing these tiny humans that fear fades when we face it together. This reminds me of my sista group, who support each other through life's toughest challenges. We celebrate even the smallest victories because sometimes, just getting out of bed and showering can feel like a huge accomplishment.

I am also reminded of the fantastic people I have met through church, DC, and our community all over the world who have held my hand and taught me that fear fades when we are brave together. Life can be challenging, but it's easier with God, family, friends, and even a personal trainer. Together, we can charge into the darkness and come out on the other side to see the most beautiful things. And for those hesitating at the water's edge, remember to extend your hand for assistance.

We never know whose life we might touch by simply being there for one another. It's these connections that make life richer and more meaningful. My journey with Elijah has taught me that even in the face of immense challenges, love, support, and a shared sense of courage can illuminate the darkest paths.

As we navigate through these uncertain times, I find solace in knowing that we are not alone. The collective strength of those around us - family, friends, and community - provides a foundation upon which we can build resilience and hope. We learn to lean on each other, to offer a shoulder to cry on and to celebrate each milestone, no matter how small.

Elijah's spirit remains unbroken, and his bucket list becomes a testament to the beauty of life, despite its brevity. Each adventure we embark on together serves as a reminder that life is to be cherished and lived fully.

And so, as we continue on this journey, let us remember that bravery is not the absence of fear, but the willingness to face it together. Let us reach out to those around us, offering our hands and hearts, and in doing so, create a tapestry of strength and compassion that can withstand any storm.

Together, we can transform fear into courage, sorrow into joy, and uncertainty into a shared journey of love and support. Let us embrace the power of togetherness and move forward with hope, knowing that the most beautiful waterfalls are often found at the end of the most challenging paths.

It's Not Usually One Single Event

It's not usually one single event that brings us down,

It's not usually one single event that brings us down, but instead, the culmination of many things that we try to handle alone until it becomes too much.

This week on our latest trip across the United States, Our morning started well! I had front-row seats to Avayha and Mackenzie's stand-up comedy show. As we stood in front of the large bathroom mirrors, they styled Avayha's hair. These girls are funny! I heard Elijah laugh at Bluey from the other room. We managed to get five mini humans, including one with medical needs, safely settled in the van with all our belongings. It felt almost too easy, with no arguments. However, suddenly, the check engine light came on, causing us to worry about the safety of our journey.

I took the time to check the fluid levels of the vehicle. We also went to the carwash to remove the tongue prints from the animal safari park that were left on the car the day before. A thought crossed my mind that the park could double its profits if it opened a carwash in the parking lot. After having the codes checked, we discovered that we had a misfire on one of the vehicle's cylinders. This is a crucial issue that needs to be addressed to ensure that the car can continue to operate safely and efficiently.

I found myself in a situation where I needed mechanical assistance and did what I always do - I decided to call my younger brother, who happens to be one of the best mechanics I know. After explaining my predicament to him, I asked the question I always ask in such situations - "How long can I wait to face this?". My brother took some time to consider the issue and came back to me with the information that I needed. He told me that, although the problem needed to be addressed eventually, I could make it to our next stop without any issues. This was important to me, as I had a plan for the day that didn't involve taking time out to deal with a vehicle problem. I was relieved to have his advice and know I could continue my plans. However, I also knew that the problem would eventually need to be addressed. This situation made me realize that sometimes in life, we encounter problems that we know need to be fixed, but they don't fit into our plans.

Well, I decided to go on with our day as planned. We stopped at the center of the universe in Tulsa, a place that has been on our bucket list for some time. As we leave, the check engine light comes back on, a reminder that something is wrong. I get several emails and phone calls about insurance equipment and feeding supplies. These are all things I would like to ignore for the next two weeks. I know they will be there when I get home.

After receiving numerous emails regarding my future and the decisions ahead, I became overwhelmed. Seeking support, I turned to my closest friends my Zoom Sisters for prayers. Then the check engine light came on again. Which led us to change our plans and stop two hours earlier than intended. Ironically, it was the last place I wanted to be - the town where I once lived with my ex-husband. While the town itself was fine, it held painful memories I hadn't fully dealt with.

Even though it was NOT where I wanted to be and NOT anywhere I would have ever planned to be! We found ourselves in a safe haven provided by God, with all our needs met and more. Kind individuals came to our aid, arranging our hotel stay and meals, and a generous mechanic fixed my van for only the cost of parts, offering his services free of charge.

Additionally, someone reached out to me with an exciting new adventure, and I talked things through with my best friend. Just like that, the burden I was carrying felt a little lighter. A few hours earlier, I had been unsure if I could go on if I was making any difference, or how I would get home, let alone complete the rest of our adventure.

Sometimes, when we feel there is no way out, help can come from unexpected places. That's what happened to us. Now, I'm sitting in a hotel room in the early morning hours, surrounded by the sound of my sleeping children and watching the sunrise over the gorgeous Texas landscape.

Life can be challenging, but we can always find hope and inspiration in the people around us. It's essential to allow others to help carry our burdens and to walk alongside us, supporting us and praying for us. We are braver together! And when warning signs appear in our lives, it's important to notice them before they become more significant problems.

As I sit here, reflecting on the past few days, I realize just how much we've been blessed by the kindness of others and the strength of our community. It's in these moments of vulnerability that we find our true resilience. The journey isn't just about reaching our physical destinations but also about the personal growth and connections we make along the way.

This trip has taught me so much about patience, faith, and the power of a supportive network. While we still have a long way to go, both in our travels and in our personal challenges, I feel a renewed sense of hope and determination. The road ahead may be uncertain, but with the love and support of those around us, I know we can navigate any obstacle.

As the sun rises higher, painting the sky with hues of pink and orange, I'm reminded of the beauty that exists even in chaos. Each day is a new opportunity to embrace the unknown, to find joy in the little things, and to lean on each other when the weight of the world feels too heavy.

To anyone reading this, remember that you are never alone in your struggles. Reach out, ask for help, and allow yourself to be vulnerable. Together, we can overcome anything. Here's to the adventures that lie ahead and the unbreakable bonds that carry us through life's toughest moments.

Letting Go

Letting go of my fears could lead me to breathtaking places.

This experience is definitely one of my favorites! Here's how it all unfolded: Initially, I wasn't keen on ziplining! This wasn't my idea of a good time. Avayha and Isaiah were eager to try it out but needed an adult to accompany them. Mike volunteered, but with only two lines available, he couldn't go with both. Consequently, the boys paired up, and so did the girls. Heights are not my thing, so this adventure was not on my agenda. I was quite hesitant at first!

We started with a trial run on a shorter line before discovering that the zipline stretched two-thirds of a mile and soared 130 feet above rhinos, giraffes, and other wildlife at the San Diego Zoo Safari Park. Harnessed up, all four of us boarded a safari truck that took us up a small mountain, passing through gates that evoked memories of Jurassic Park. My heart pounded as we reached the platform. Mike and Isaiah bravely took the lead, making my fears seem insignificant.

Despite my apprehension, I made up my mind to confront it head-on. I chose to be scared but take the leap anyway! As Avayha and I prepared, the countdown commenced, and my nerves peaked. I doubted if I could release the hook on my own. However, once I was launched and glided over the animals, I quickly realized it was one of the best decisions I've ever made.

As I soared over the magnificent animals at the San Diego Zoo Safari Park, a sense of liberation washed over me, replacing my initial fear with pure excitement. The feeling of gliding through the air, surrounded by nature's beauty and the sounds of the wild, was truly unforgettable.

The zipline felt like a metaphor for life itself - taking risks, stepping out of your comfort zone, and reaping the rewards of facing your fears. The experience taught me a valuable lesson about the power of pushing past my limits and embracing new challenges with courage. Being afraid and doing it anyway.

Reflecting on this adventure, I realized that sometimes the most rewarding experiences come from saying "yes" to the unknown and embracing the opportunities that come our way. The memories of that day continue to inspire me to seek out more adventures and embrace the thrill of the unknown with open arms.

The exhilaration of that first zipline ride has ignited a newfound passion within me. Every time I think back to that day, I can almost feel the rush of wind against my face and the breathtaking view of the park below. Since then, I have been actively seeking out new ziplining spots, each one offering its own unique scenery and challenges.

This experience has not only made me a zipline enthusiast but has also encouraged Isaiah to explore other adventure activities. he has started to build a bucket list that includes everything from paragliding in the Swiss Alps to bungee jumping off the Kawarau Bridge in New Zealand. Each activity represents a new opportunity to confront fears and embrace the thrill of the unknown.

In many ways, ziplining has become a symbol of my commitment to living life to the fullest. It serves as a reminder that sometimes, the best moments come from stepping outside the familiar and daring to try something new. Whether it's gliding over a dense forest or simply taking a new path in life, the spirit of adventure and the courage to face my fears will always guide me.

Who knows what the future holds? What I do know is that I am ready to face it head-on, with the same excitement and bravery that I found on that zipline. Life is too short to let fear dictate our choices. So, here's to more adventures, more memories, and more moments that take our breath away!

Before The Craziness

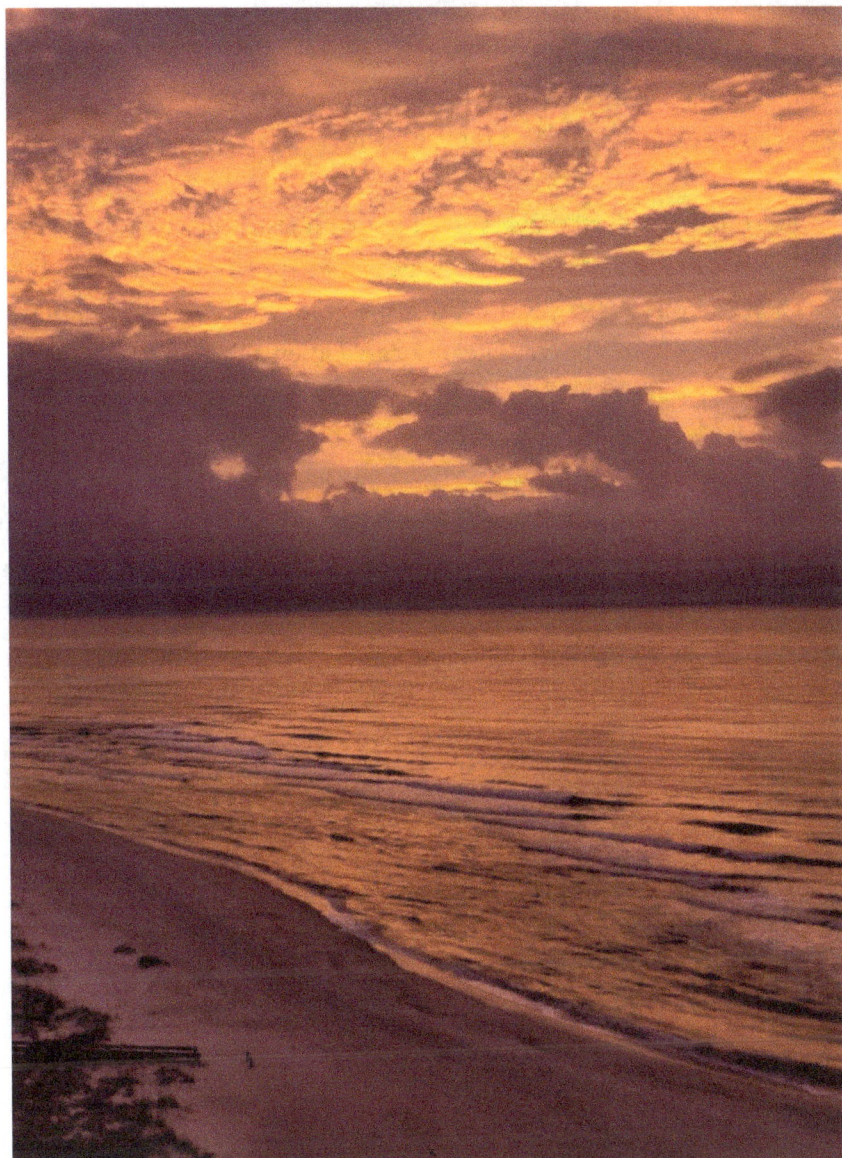

Before the craziness of the day begins.

Starting each day with a specific routine can be a wise decision that sets the tone for a positive and productive day. As my dear friend once said, it's best to begin by waking up, praying, and working. This way, we prioritize our spiritual connection with God above everything else.

Personally, I still start every morning with Jesus and coffee. I believe that beginning each day with gratitude is key to living a fulfilling life. As soon as I open my eyes, I express my gratitude to God for another day: my family, my home, and my car. I then make my way to the kitchen and start all the fantastic machines that make my life easier, starting with the coffee maker!

As I savor my morning coffee in the peaceful hours before the craziness of the day begins, I take time to talk to God and pour out all my worries to Him. It's an excellent feeling to let go and give my troubles to God. Then, for the rest of the day, if worry starts to intrude, I remind myself that I already gave those worries to God. Most of the time, things are never as bad as I imagine them to be. And God has a way of working things out, even if I don't see a way!

As the aroma of freshly brewed coffee fills the air, I find solace in the stillness of the morning. With each sip, I feel a sense of peace wash over me, grounding me for the day ahead. The quiet moments spent in reflection and prayer set the stage for a day filled with positivity and purpose.

After my morning routine, I tackle the day with renewed energy and a grateful heart. I carry with me the assurance that I am not alone in facing any challenges that may come my way. With faith as my guide, I navigate through the day's ups and downs, knowing that I am supported by a higher power.

Through the hustle and bustle of the day, I hold onto the serenity of those early morning moments. The simple act of starting each day with Jesus and coffee serves as a reminder of the blessings that surround me. In moments of doubt or stress, I draw strength from the belief that everything will work out in the end, guided by a force greater than myself.

So, as I take on each day with a heart full of gratitude and a spirit lifted by faith, I find joy in the knowledge that I am part of something much larger and more profound. And with each sunrise, I am reminded of the endless possibilities that lie ahead, fueled by my connection to something greater than myself.

Embracing this morning ritual has transformed the way I experience life. It has taught me the importance of mindfulness and the power of small, consistent actions in crafting a meaningful existence. Whether it's the quiet moments of prayer, the warmth of the coffee cup in my hands, or the reassuring sense of divine presence, each element of my routine serves as a cornerstone of my well-being.

As the day unfolds, this foundation of gratitude and faith empowers me to approach challenges with a calm and centered mindset. It reminds me to be patient with myself and others, to listen more intently, and to act with kindness and compassion. The simple act of starting my day with intention has a ripple effect, influencing every interaction and decision I make.

In a world that often feels chaotic and overwhelming, these morning moments offer a sanctuary—a place where I can reconnect with my core values and set a positive trajectory for the hours ahead. They remind me of the beauty in simplicity and the profound impact of nurturing my spiritual and emotional health.

And so, I continue this practice, day after day, finding strength in its consistency and comfort in its familiarity. It is a daily testament to the power of faith, gratitude, and intentional living. With each new dawn, I am reminded that I have the choice to start afresh, to embrace the opportunities that lie before me, and to live each day with a heart full of love and a spirit grounded in peace.

Finding Joy

If you choose not to find joy
in the snow, you will have
less joy in your life but still
the same amount of snow!

ELIJAHSBABYBUCKETLIST.COM

Finding Joy

I woke up this morning to snow, like many others. However, I wasn't too thrilled about it. My younger sister sent me a quote that read, "If you choose not to find joy in the snow, you will have less joy in your life but still the same amount of snow." Don't get me wrong; I still find joy in snow falling soundlessly in the middle of the night but working in it is a different story. During Christmas, I work long hours at the Post Office, which means poor driving conditions and the need to shovel. I am not looking forward to that. But today is different. Today, I get to work from home and make fantastic memories with my mini humans.

When I woke my ten-year-old son, he jumped out of bed and ran to the window. Isaiah was overflowing with joy and excitement over an inch of snow. I started my coffee and began unloading the dryer. As I headed to the bedroom with the basket, there was always an overabundance of laundry. I could hear him like the town crier announcing to our still-silent sleeping house that it had snowed! He almost tipped over as he wiggled into the snow pants he had sat out the night before. Some of his older sisters have lost that excitement for the first snow. And I started to wonder. When did I lose that "Jump out of bed on fire" love in my life?

I don't think the quote was written to have any religious meaning, but it reminds me of Philippians 4:4: "Rejoice in the Lord always; again, I will say rejoice." James goes on to say, "Consider it all joy, my brothers, when you encounter various trials." The implication is that we should find joy, not just in mundane things like snow but also in trials, sickness, and hardships. It's much easier to say or read these words than to put them into practice. How does one find joy in laundry, the heartache of divorce, sickness, and snow?

When we get enough snow, we must slow down. As travel is disrupted and school is canceled, it causes us to take a step back to smell the coffee and build a snowman. Let's face it: who can deny the snuggle power of snow? After a day of sledding, snow angels, and snowball fights, there is nothing like cuddling up with my mini-humans and a cup of hot cocoa. Perhaps the most beautiful aspect of snow and heart-ache is that it is fleeting. As the temperature rises and the ground thaws, the former world we know will be revealed once more, creating yet another new beginning for us to appreciate.

As the snow continued to fall gently outside, I couldn't help but reflect on the profound words my younger sister had shared with me earlier. It made me pause and consider the different ways we can choose to approach the challenges and joys that come our way. Watching my son, Isaiah, burst with pure delight at the sight of the snow reminded me of the simple beauty in finding joy in the little things.

With a fresh perspective, I carried on with my day, embracing the coziness of working from home and the extra time spent with my kids. The laundry seemed never-ending, but Isaiah's infectious enthusiasm kept the atmosphere light and joyful. I realized that perhaps the key to rediscovering that "jump out of bed on fire" love lies in finding joy in the present moment, regardless of the circumstances.

Just like the verse from Philippians and the quote about snow, I understood that true joy can be found not only in moments of happiness but also in times of trial and difficulty. It's a challenging concept to grasp, but as I navigated through the day, I found solace in the idea that even amidst life's messiness, there is beauty to be found.

As the day unfolded, filled with snowball fights and laughter, I embraced the temporary nature of both the snow outside and the struggles we face. Just as the snow eventually melts away, paving the way for new beginnings, I held onto the hope that every challenge we encounter is an opportunity for growth and resilience.

So, as I sat down with my family, sipping on hot cocoa and basking in the warmth of togetherness, I made a silent vow to always seek joy in the midst of life's chaos. After all, just like the snow that blankets the ground, our moments of hardship are fleeting, leaving behind a fresh canvas for us to paint with love, gratitude, and unwavering joy. I pray I always find joy in my hot mess!

Be Still

Be Still.

"For I know the plans I have for you," declares the Lord, "plans to prosper you and not to harm you, plans to give you hope and a future."

This verse from Jeremiah 29:11 is one that I am very familiar with, even before I had a relationship with God.

But now, as I parent my kids, I understand it better. One of my children, who is 12 years old, reminds me a lot of myself. She wants to know every single detail of our upcoming adventures. Although she is always grateful for whatever I give her, as her mom, I always want to provide her with more than just what she asks for, more than what she even knows exists outside of her "reality."

She doesn't know so much about life yet, but like me, she wants a plan. She wants to know what is coming, but I enjoy a good surprise sometimes. So, I only share things with her when it is time. Recently, she expressed interest in reborn dolls. I told her to wait and we will look at them. However, she was unsatisfied with that and started formulating a plan to get one for herself.

I had planned to take her to a store so that she could look at them and pick one in person. She doesn't know this yet, but I prefer to surprise her and see her joy when things work out. She saved her money and worked very hard to buy a cheaper version from Amazon. It was not the one she initially wanted, but she said it worked. Unfortunately, it was poorly made, and the head fell off, making it rather creepy-looking.

I told her that, as her momma, I am always working things out in the background, and she needs to be still. It hit me like a ton of bricks; how often have I needed something to work out a certain way? I wanted that thing or needed to figure out how I would do something. BUT GOD! He knew he was working things out in the background while I cried, obsessed, and worried. While I worked, googled, and tried to figure out how I would make a way, He was making a way where there was "no way"!

I realized that as a parent, I understand this verse better and appreciate surprises that bring joy to my child. It reminds me that sometimes, I need to be still and watch what God does rather than obsessing and worrying about how I will make a way. God is always working things out in the background, making a way where there seems to be no way. I should stop fighting and trust in His plans for us.

And so, I decided to lean into this newfound understanding, embracing the patience and trust that come with it. Each day, I remind myself to take a step back and allow things to unfold in their own time, just as I want my daughter to experience the delight of unexpected blessings.

As we navigate this journey together, I see the parallels in our lives—how she mirrors my desires for control and certainty, and how I must guide her gently towards faith and trust. I know that these lessons will not only shape her character but also deepen our bond as she learns that her momma, much like God, has her best interests at heart.

In the quiet moments of reflection, I pray for the wisdom to parent with grace and the strength to model the very trust I wish to instill in her. Life's unpredictability becomes a canvas for God's intricate designs, and I am learning to appreciate the beauty in the unknown.

As my daughter matures, I hope she will look back and see the love woven into every surprise, the care in every unspoken plan, and the joy in discovering that sometimes the best gifts are the ones we didn't see coming. Through it all, I aim to teach her that while she may not always see the path ahead, she can rest assured that it is paved with love, faith, and divine purpose.

I believe that this journey of parenting will not only mold her but also refine me. Each day presents new opportunities to trust more deeply, to love more freely, and to embrace the unexpected with open arms. We are learning together, my daughter and I, navigating the delicate balance between planning and letting go.

As we share our lives, I find solace in the fact that life's greatest lessons often come wrapped in ordinary moments—those bedtime talks, the shared laughter, and even the tears. She teaches me as much as I teach her, perhaps even more. Her curiosity, her eagerness to understand the world, and her innocent faith remind me to look at life with a sense of wonder and trust.

In the end, I want her to know that life, with all its twists and turns, is a beautiful journey. And while it may not always follow the map we have in mind, it always leads us to where we need to be. Together, we will continue to discover the joys of the unexpected and the profound peace that comes from trusting in a greater plan.

So, as I tuck her in at night and whisper a prayer over her, I hold onto the hope that she will grow into a woman who embodies faith, resilience, and an unwavering belief in the goodness that surrounds us. For now, I cherish these moments, these lessons, and the incredible privilege of watching her grow.

Unknowing

Unknowing.

There are times when I feel overwhelmed and have no idea how to handle a situation. It is during such times that I find myself turning to

God for help. When everything seems complex and chaotic, and I feel like I am struggling to keep things together, I call out to Him from the depths of my heart.

Prayer is my lifeline, but sometimes it is a little rushed, or I don't put my heart into it. However, I always remember that I cannot do it alone. When I am in a dark place or struggling with something, I cry out to God and tell Him that I cannot do it alone.

He reminds me that He knows and that I was never meant to do it alone. All I need to do is reach out and ask for help. So, the next time you are unsure about what to do or where to start, realize that it is okay not to. Know that you belong in that place of unknowing and that God is always there to help you.

He is a constant presence, ready to offer guidance and strength. It is in these moments of vulnerability and humility that we often find our greatest growth. By admitting our limitations and seeking divine assistance, we open ourselves to a deeper connection with God and a clearer understanding of our path.

In addition to prayer, reflecting on scripture and immersing ourselves in the stories of faith can bring comfort and direction. The Bible is filled with accounts of individuals who faced immense challenges, yet found solace and solutions through their faith. These narratives remind us that we are not alone in our struggles and that there is always hope.

Surrounding ourselves with a supportive community can provide additional strength. Whether it's a faith group, friends, or family, an online community, a support group, sharing our burdens with others can lighten the load and offer new perspectives. Just as God is there to support us, so too are those who care about us.

Remember, it's okay to feel overwhelmed and unsure. These feelings are part of the human experience. What matters is how we respond to them. By turning to God, seeking His wisdom, and leaning on our community, we can navigate even the most daunting challenges.

So, take a deep breath, trust in His plan, and know that with faith, you can find peace and clarity. Embrace the journey with an open heart, and you will discover the strength and courage needed to overcome any obstacle.

Life is a journey filled with ups and downs, and it's during the most uncertain times that we often discover our true resilience. Embracing the unknown with faith not only fortifies our spirit but also helps us grow in ways we never imagined.

Every step we take in faith, even when the path is unclear, brings us closer to the divine purpose laid out for us. Trusting in God's timing and wisdom can transform our perspective, turning what seems like a daunting challenge into an opportunity for profound growth and understanding.

In moments of doubt, remember that each experience, whether joyous or painful, contributes to the tapestry of our lives. These experiences shape us, teach us, and prepare us for the future. By leaning into faith and maintaining an open heart, we allow ourselves to be guided by a higher power that knows our needs and desires more intimately than we do.

As we continue this journey, let us remain mindful of the blessings that come our way, even those disguised as challenges. Let us cultivate gratitude for the lessons learned and the strength gained. Through faith, prayer, and community, we can navigate the complexities of life with grace and resilience.

So, whenever you find yourself standing at the crossroads of uncertainty, hold steadfast to your faith. Trust that you are exactly where you need to be and that every step forward is a step toward becoming the person you are meant to be. With each prayer, each act of kindness, and each moment of reflection, you build a life rooted in love, faith, and purpose.

May you continue to find peace in the unknown, strength in your faith, and joy in the journey.

The Joy of The Lord Is My Strength

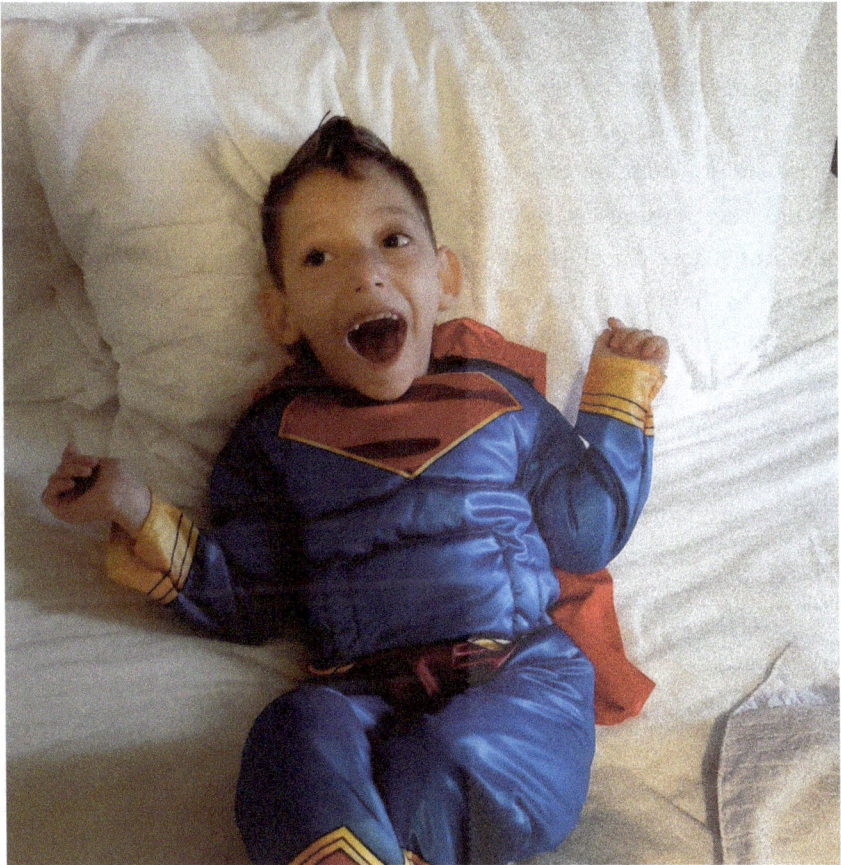

The Joy of The Lord Is My Strength.

Living for the Lord is my calling. I am not waiting for God to heal my son. Instead, I have learned to embrace my faith and live out loud.

It is all about how you perceive your story. Joy is not just a spiritual fruit, but also a spiritual force. Nehemiah 8:10 demonstrates the power of joy by stating that the joy of the Lord is your strength. God wants you to use this spiritual force as a weapon to face the difficulties you may be experiencing in life.

Don't believe the misconception that joy can only be found in a pain-free life. Instead, celebrate the process, not just the outcome, and cultivate gratitude for what remains, no matter how small it may seem. Psalm 16:6 reminds us that "the boundary lines have fallen for me in pleasant places; surely I have a delightful inheritance." This scripture speaks to the importance of recognizing and appreciating the blessings and opportunities that surround us, even in the midst of challenges.

It's essential to remember that our trials do not define us, but rather, how we respond to them shapes our journey. Embracing joy and gratitude can transform our perspective and empower us to rise above our circumstances. Each day, find moments to celebrate the victories, no matter how minor they appear, and let those moments fortify your spirit.

Surround yourself with a community that uplifts and supports you. Share your experiences and allow others to share theirs. This exchange of stories can foster a sense of connection and remind us that we are never alone in our struggles.

Ultimately, living for the Lord means embodying His love, grace, and joy in every aspect of our lives. It means trusting in His plan and finding strength in His promises, even when the path ahead is uncertain. Let your faith shine brightly, illuminating the way for others and inspiring them to discover the strength and joy that come from a life rooted in God's love.

In moments of doubt and hardship, turn to prayer and reflection, seeking solace in the divine presence that guides you. It's in these quiet moments that we often find the clarity and courage to continue our journey with renewed vigor. The scriptures provide a wellspring of wisdom and comfort, reminding us of the unwavering love that God has for each of us.

As you navigate the complexities of life, let your faith be a beacon of hope not just for yourself, but for those around you. Your resilience and determination can serve as a powerful testimony to the transformative power of faith. By living with purpose and intention, you can inspire others to embrace their own spiritual journey with confidence and joy.

Remember that every challenge you face is an opportunity for growth and a chance to deepen your relationship with God. Embrace the lessons that come your way, and trust that each step you take is part of a greater plan, one that is filled with promise and potential.

May your heart be filled with peace and your spirit be lifted, knowing that you are held in the loving arms of the Creator. Continue to live boldly, with a heart full of gratitude and a soul alight with the joy of the Lord. Your life is a testament to the enduring power of faith, and through your journey, you are planting seeds of hope and love that will blossom in the hearts of many.

Balance

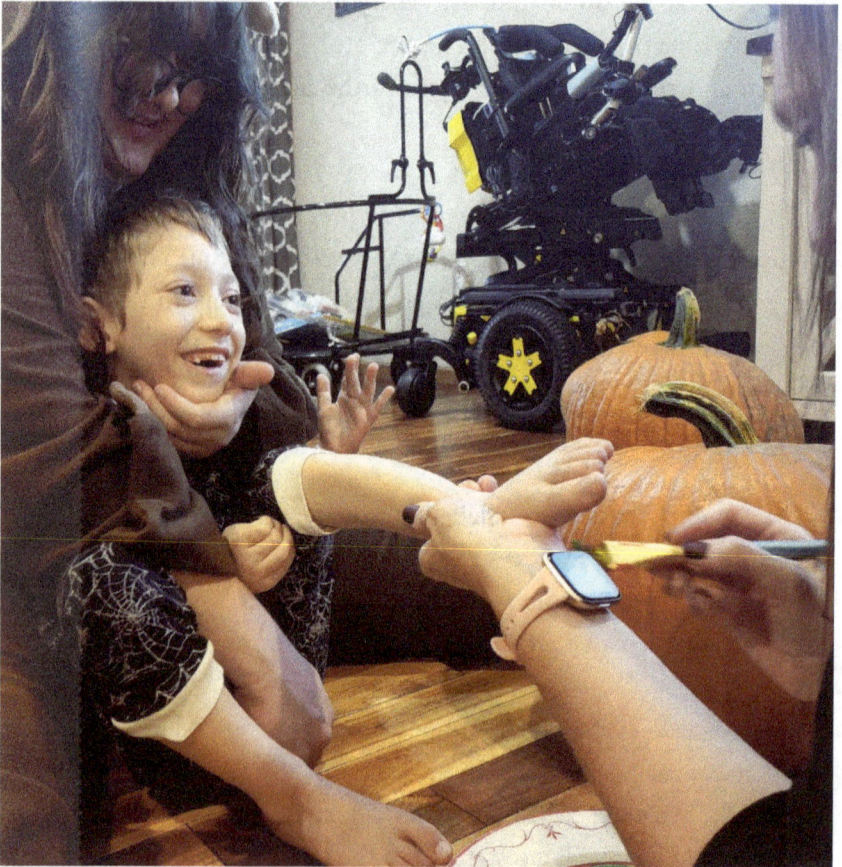

Balance.

Today, we had a fantastic time carving and painting pumpkins, with each of us bringing our unique creativity. The laughter and chatter that filled the room were music to my ears, and the sweet smell of pumpkin and paint was a sensory delight. However, amidst all the joy, holidays can get overwhelming for me. As I strive to create everlasting memories for my mini-humans, I am also confronted with the reality of anticipatory grief and the transitory nature of life.

Living with Elijah's terminal diagnosis, I am constantly reminded of the fragility of life, and it can be challenging to balance the desire to celebrate with the sad thoughts of the future. But his infectious enthusiasm never fails to lift my spirits. His innocent giggles and the joy he exuded while watching the antics as his siblings carved pumpkins were a reminder of the importance of living in the present.

He has taught me to find happiness in every moment, no matter how fleeting, and to cherish every memory like a unique treasure.

As the evening drew to a close, we gathered around the flickering candlelight in the smiling jack-o-lanterns, sharing stories and sipping on hot cocoa. Elijah nestled into my lap, his eyes twinkling with excitement. His siblings sat close by, their faces illuminated by the warm glow of the candlelight in the pumpkins a scene that felt both comforting and bittersweet.

In these moments, I am profoundly grateful for the time we have together. The simple joys—like the laughter that erupted when someone's pumpkin turned out more comical than scary, or the way Elijah's eyes lit up at the sight of his finished creation—become the pillars that hold us up, even when the weight of uncertainty presses down.

I realize that while I cannot change the future, I can fill our present with love, laughter, and as many happy memories as possible. The stories we share, the smiles we exchange, and the small acts of kindness that echo through our days are what truly matter.

As I tucked Elijah and Isaiah into bed that night, Elijah's little hand in mine, Isaiah whispered, "I had the best day, Mom." And in that moment, all the worries and fears faded into the background, replaced by a profound sense of peace and fulfillment. We are living, truly living, and that is the greatest gift of all.

Perseverance

Perseverance

Let's delve into Perseverance, which entails maintaining persistence and not giving up, especially when faced with challenges or setbacks on the path to success. As Walter Elliot stated, "Perseverance is not a long race; it is many short races one after the other." This week, I experienced this firsthand as I tackled one challenge after another, reminding myself that progress comes from continuous forward movement. The unwavering support, encouragement, coffee, and reminders from those around me were invaluable in navigating through these hurdles.

This brings me to Philippians! I'm truly amazed by the dedication of a close friend who memorized the entire book of Philippians. The commitment and effort she put into this achievement are truly commendable. Her flawless recitation gives the impression that she is quoting directly from the Bible. Her faith, perseverance, and steadfast commitment are truly inspiring, unlike my struggle with remembering names. I didn't remember signing up for a Tuesday night bible study until Wednesday morning. I am a hot mess!

She motivated me to memorize this verse: "Do not worry about anything; instead, pray about everything. Tell God what you need, and thank him for all he has done. Then, you will experience God's peace, which exceeds anything we can understand. His peace will guard your hearts and minds as you live in Christ Jesus." -Philippians 4:6-7

Meanwhile, I've decided to take small steps to enhance my memory by using a journal for important dates and setting reminders on my phone. It's a work in progress, but these changes hold the promise of significant improvement.

As the day draws to a close, I find myself contemplating the numerous blessings in my life, from the simple joy of a warm cup of coffee to the profound impact of supportive loved ones. Despite life's challenges, these moments of beauty and grace make the journey meaningful.

Let's embrace each day with gratitude and perseverance, finding the strength to move forward and the wisdom to cherish life's simple pleasures. And yes, I'll definitely celebrate if I remember to attend Bible study on Tuesday!

The Fall

The Fall

Isaiah and I had the pleasure of spending some quality time together to celebrate his birthday. We decided to stop by our favorite coffee shop, and he indulged in his favorite drink. As we approached the window to pay, the friendly baristas were thrilled to learn that it was

Isaiah's birthday and gave him his drink for free. His excitement was palpable, and he couldn't stop grinning from ear to ear.

Afterward, we made an unexpected stop at Subway. This year, Isaiah had outgrown the traditional Happy Meal from McDonald's, so he was thrilled to be able to create his sandwich exactly how he wanted it. To our surprise, the kind staff at Subway also gave him a cookie to celebrate his special day.

We then headed to the park to enjoy our lunch and chat. We savored the beautiful weather and admired the picturesque scenery around us. Isaiah was having the time of his life, exclaiming that it was the best birthday he had ever had. Unfortunately, his joy was short-lived.

After finishing our meal, he cleared the table and eagerly asked if he could play on the playground. I happily granted his request. How many birthdays will I get to spend at the park with him? I watched him make a beeline for the zip line, which has always been his favorite attraction.

As he climbed up to the starting point, I couldn't help but reminisce about the countless times I had lifted him so he could reach the handle. But now, he is almost grown and no longer needs my assistance. With a determined look on his face, he grabbed the handle and launched himself forward with all his might.

However, something went terribly wrong. The handle caught, and my heart sank as I realized that he was hurtling towards the ground at breakneck speed. As a student of science, I knew all too well about the principle of inertia - a body in motion stays in motion until an external force acts upon it. Unfortunately, the force that stopped his motion was the unforgiving ground, and he landed with a sickening thud on his back.

I hurried over to him, taking quick strides as I noticed he wasn't moving or making any sounds. He looked petrified, and I immediately knew he had knocked the wind out of himself. His tiny voice called out for help, saying he couldn't breathe. I stood beside him, gently laying my hand on his shoulder and reassuring him to stay calm. I suggested he try sitting upright and taking slow, deep breaths, inhaling and exhaling as calmly as possible. Tears streamed down his face as I asked if he was hurt anywhere else. He mentioned a few scrapes on his back from the collision with the wood chips, but his breathing was still labored.

I mirrored slow, deep breaths, and finally, he was able to inhale deeply and breathe normally once again. We slowly made our way to the car, and he lamented that this was "the worst birthday he'd ever had." I asked him if it really was, and he began to cry again, saying, "It wasn't the worst, but that part of it was terrible!" He said, "Sometimes, bad things happen, but it doesn't cancel out the good things." He thanked me for "Being there to help him breathe again.", and I felt a sense of relief and pride.

It's hard to put into words just how much that statement resonates with me. Countless moments in life feel exactly like that - like the wind has been knocked right out of you. I recall feeling that way after my divorce, and even now, with Elijah's diagnosis, there are still times when I feel like I can't catch my breath. But every time, without fail, someone shows up like a beacon of light and helps me find my breath once more. They can't take away the pain or breathe for me, but their support means everything. They walk alongside me and encourage me to look to Jesus when nothing seems to make sense. I need that! All of it!

It's crucial to remember that when things are tough and the pain feels unbearable, it doesn't negate all the beautiful things in life. It's just a bump in the road, and it's okay to take a moment to lie there and process it all. It's okay to feel overwhelmed for a moment, but then we must find our breath and focus on the lessons that come with the hardships that knock the wind out of us.

As we drove home, the atmosphere in the car gradually shifted from somber to serene. Isaiah, still a bit shaken but resilient as ever, began to recount the highlights of his day. His face lit up as he spoke about the free coffee, the custom sandwich, and the cookie from Subway. Despite the mishap, he chose to remember the joy and kindness he had experienced.

Later that evening, as I tucked Isaiah into bed, he held my hand tightly and whispered, "Thank you for making my birthday special." I kissed his forehead and reminded him of how proud I was of his courage and positivity. I told him that every moment, whether good or bad, adds to the beautiful tapestry of his life, and that he should cherish them all.

As I closed his bedroom door, I reflected on the day's events. Isaiah had unknowingly given me a profound lesson: that resilience and gratitude can transform even the most challenging experiences into valuable memories. It was a reminder that in the face of adversity, it's the love and support we share that helps us find our breath and keeps us moving forward.

The next morning, Isaiah woke up with renewed enthusiasm, eagerly planning what adventures we might embark on next. His spirit was a testament to the incredible capacity children have to bounce back from setbacks and embrace life with unbridled joy. As his parent, I felt immensely grateful for the opportunity to witness and nurture that resilience.

In the days that followed, I found myself more mindful of the small moments of happiness and connection that often go unnoticed. Whether it was a shared laugh over breakfast, a spontaneous hug, or a quiet moment of reflection, each one felt like a precious gift. And through it all, I held on to the wisdom that Isaiah had inadvertently shared with me: life's challenges may knock the wind out of us, but with love, support, and a positive outlook, we can always find our breath again.

Divine Narrative

It became clear to me that this was not just any story but rather a divine narrative.

I bet you've experienced moments when a quote or a message on a mug caught your attention and triggered memories or emotions.

85

That happened to me this morning as I was sipping my coffee. The inscription on my mug reads, "Remember why you started," it took me back to a difficult time when my son Elijah was just nine months old. Medical experts predicted he wouldn't make it past his second birthday, and that news was devastating.

But instead of giving up, I decided to make the most of the time we had left with him. We went on our first epic adventure. As I sat on the peaceful beach with my other children, we started discussing Elijah's bucket list and how we could make the most of the limited time we had left with him. We started Elijah's Baby Bucket List. We go on trips and try to enjoy every moment. And you know what? Something amazing happened. As we traveled, we discovered that the world was just as eager to see Elijah as we were to show him everything it had to offer. His laughter and smile brought so much joy to everyone he met.

Watching my son taught me the true meaning of joy and unconditional love, and I'm grateful. As I began to reflect on the events that unfolded, I came to a sudden realization that the series of coincidences and twists of fate that brought us to this point was not merely a matter of chance but rather a part of a grander scheme. It became clear to me that this was not just any story but rather a divine narrative, with each of us playing a significant role in its unfolding. It was a humbling experience to recognize that we are a part of something bigger than ourselves. It filled me with a sense of awe and reverence to know that we were all part of God's plan.

My perspective on life shifted dramatically, and I began to see every day as a precious gift. Elijah has defied the odds, and as he has grown older, his strength and resilience have become a beacon of hope for our family and everyone who hears our story. The doctors who once gave us such grim news are astounded by his progress, and Elijah's journey has become a source of inspiration far beyond our immediate circle.

We continue to add to Elijah's Baby Bucket List, each new adventure a testament to the power of love, faith, and community. From mountain coaster rides to meeting his favorite storybook characters, every experience is cherished, not just for Elijah, but for all of us. We learn to find joy in the little things—a sunny day, a shared laugh, a quiet moment by the fire.

As Elijah's story spreads, we are overwhelmed by the support and kindness of strangers. People from all walks of life reach out to us, sharing their own stories of hope and resilience. This network of love and solidarity has become a lifeline, reminding us that we are never truly alone.

In the end, Elijah's life is filled with more love and joy than many experience in a lifetime. He continues to remind us of the incredible strength of the human spirit and the profound impact of living each day with purpose and gratitude.

So, when I see the words "Remember why you started" on my coffee mug, I am reminded of the incredible journey we embarked on with Elijah—a journey that is teaching us the true essence of life and the unyielding power of love. And I carry that lesson with me every single day, knowing that no matter what challenges come our way, we have the strength to overcome them and the grace to find beauty in the midst of it all.

Rock Bottom

Rock Bottom!

Have you ever found yourself in a situation where everything seems to be falling apart, and you feel like you have hit rock bottom? It can be an extremely challenging and emotional experience that can leave you feeling lost, hopeless, and helpless. However, you should know that hitting rock bottom does not signify the end of your journey. In fact, it can be a turning point, a chance to reflect on your life and relationships and figure out what is truly important to you.

When you are caught up in the daily grind, it's easy to lose sight of your core values, passions, and priorities. But hitting rock bottom can be a wake-up call, a moment of clarity that helps you shift your focus back to what matters most. It can be a transformative experience that helps you grow and learn from your mistakes. Although the journey ahead may be tough, it's an opportunity to start anew and create a better future for yourself.

It's important to understand that hitting rock bottom doesn't define you. Instead, it's an opportunity to take a step back, re-evaluate your life, and make positive changes. You can use this experience to develop a deeper understanding of yourself, practice self-care, and work on creating a more fulfilling and meaningful life. It's a chance to shed the things that are holding you back and start fresh.

Remember, hitting rock bottom is not the end. It is simply a turning point that can lead to a brighter future. With the right mindset, tools, and support, you can emerge from this experience stronger, wiser, and more resilient than ever before. So don't give up hope. Instead, embrace this moment as an opportunity for growth and transformation.

Surround yourself with positive influences, whether that means seeking support from loved ones, joining a community group, or even engaging with a therapist or counselor. These connections can provide the encouragement and perspective you need to navigate through tough times.

Additionally, focus on setting small, achievable goals to rebuild your confidence and sense of accomplishment. Celebrate each milestone, no matter how minor it may seem, as these victories will gradually help you regain your strength and motivation. Remember to be patient with yourself—healing and growth take time.

Engage in activities that bring you joy and fulfillment. Whether it's picking up a hobby you love, spending time in nature, or practicing mindfulness and meditation, these activities can help you reconnect with your inner self and find peace amidst the chaos.

Lastly, always keep in mind that your worth is not determined by a single moment or experience. You are a complex, multifaceted individual with the capacity to overcome challenges and thrive. By embracing resilience and maintaining a hopeful outlook, you can turn the darkest times into a foundation for a brighter, more fulfilling future.

So, take a deep breath, believe in your capacity to transform, and take that first step towards rebuilding your life. You have the power to create the change you seek, and your journey from rock bottom can be the beginning of a beautiful, empowering transformation.

Burning Bush

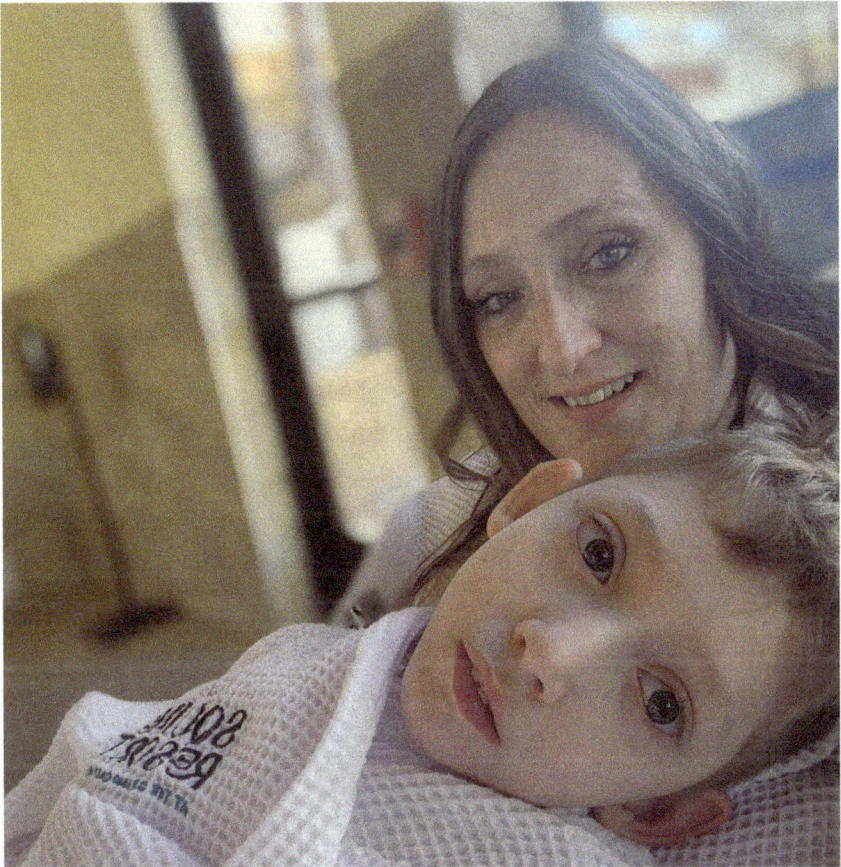

Burning Bush.

I once had a man tell me that telling my story of how I found God was harmful. Because"The people whose moms did not wake up would be pushed away from God." I am flattered and concerned that he thinks I have that much power.

Because in my eyes, God uses ALL things for those who love him. My intention is never to hurt anyone but only testify to how God shows up in my life. I have read stories far crazier about the same God. But I don't think they should have been pulled out because God does not talk to me through a burning bush. Or the fact that he has never physically parted a sea for me.

However, I have witnessed Him move mountains to bring my dear friend and her children home from Columbia at the beginning of the COVID pandemic. Don't get me wrong. There are SO many prayers I thought went unanswered. But just like other people in my life and the bible, when I look back, I can see that it happened because God protected them from someone or something.

When we don't share God's actions, we try to control who gets to hear what he can do. Imagine if someone told Moses, "Bro, don't tell people what God did because he doesn't do that for everyone." I have wept with people who have lost their kids far too soon. I have shared dinner with people who still have their mothers, and I will not stop sharing all the miracles God does in my life.

One, because there is no other way to explain some of the things he has done, and two, maybe me telling you how he shows up and you see it firsthand is what needs to happen for him to reach you or someone you know! I should not have been able to get pregnant with Elijah. His dad did chemo and radiation, which makes that impossible. Elijah was so tiny. The chances of him living and going home with me in 4 days and never needing oxygen are so small. He is deaf but has regained some of his hearing. He was given two years to live but has surpassed EVERYTHING they said he would do and turns six in January. He is not a "vegetable" and can talk!

For me, I try not to worry about anything. Sometimes, that doesn't work, but I try to remember that the God of the universe is friendly, loving, caring, and consistently performing miracles. All I need to do is look for him. I will keep sharing all the blessings God does in my life in hopes that you don't ever have to talk to a burning bush or see one of those winged multi-eye guys! Because I don't know about you, I would not be okay with either! I hope you see God in someone's story today!

And if you do, I hope it fills you with a sense of wonder and peace, knowing that there is a higher power at work, orchestrating the symphony of our lives in ways we may never fully comprehend. Each story, each miracle, is a thread in the grand tapestry of existence, weaving together moments of joy, sorrow, triumph, and faith.

It's important to remember that everyone's journey with God is unique. Some may experience grand, awe-inspiring miracles, while others may notice His presence in the small, everyday moments. Both are equally significant and worthy of being shared. It's through these stories that we can find connection, hope, and understanding.

So, whether it's a miraculous healing, an unexpected blessing, or simply the comfort of feeling God's presence during a difficult time, don't hesitate to share your experiences. You never know who might need to hear your story, who might find solace and inspiration in your words.

Let us continue to be a light for one another, sharing the beauty and power of God's work in our lives. And as we do, may we always remain open to the countless ways He reveals Himself to us, ever grateful for His boundless love and grace.

Weeds or Wishes

Weeds or Wishes?

Today, as I ran, I noticed we are in the midst of dandelion season. One day, they just show up without notice and take over. To some people, they are a nuisance, but to others, they are beautiful.

For as long as I can remember, my kids have proudly presented me with a bright yellow dandelion bouquet or a single stem in a glass proudly situated on the kitchen table, waiting for my heartfelt reaction.

Their gesture is a symbol of love that will soon wither away until the next time I wait too long to mow.

Most people do everything possible to avoid dandelions. We weed them, spray them, and hope they never return, but they always seem to show up again when we least expect it, and it's a challenge to keep our surroundings dandelion-free.

In life, we all face unwelcome challenges that we must decide to either conquer or ignore. We may feel isolated and weary, and despite our best efforts, we can't overcome them. However, life lessons are always learned if we look hard enough.

If we begin to see these challenges or hurdles as blessings or wishes, we can emerge from them stronger than before. Sometimes, climbing a mountain and finding someone to collect wishes with is the answer to our prayers.

The choice is ours to view dandelions as weeds or wishes. Wishes bring hope, hope brings perseverance, perseverance conquers challenges, and unexpected blessings become gifts.

Perhaps, the way we perceive dandelions is a reflection of our outlook on life. Just as a field of dandelions can be seen as a nuisance or a place of possibility, so too can the obstacles we face. It is a matter of perspective, a choice we make every day.

When I see my children sprinting across the yard, their laughter filling the air as they chase after dandelion seeds floating on the breeze, I am reminded of the simple joys that often go unnoticed. Their innocence and delight in such a small wonder teach me to appreciate the fleeting moments that make life beautiful.

So, the next time you find yourself surrounded by challenges, take a moment to pause and reconsider. Could these challenges be opportunities in disguise? Can you find beauty in the unexpected and joy in the small victories?

Life, like a field of dandelions, is full of surprises. Some may be unwelcome, but others might just be the wishes we never knew we needed. Embrace the dandelions, and let each one be a reminder of the endless possibilities that await.

Dandelions can either be wishes or weeds. I choose to see them as wishes. The next time you encounter a field filled with dandelions, will you pick weeds or wishes?

As you ponder this question, remember that the power lies within you to shape your experiences and outlook. Life offers us countless opportunities to redefine what we encounter. Each challenge, like a dandelion, holds the potential to be transformed into something beautiful and meaningful.

Imagine a world where we all choose to see wishes instead of weeds. How much more vibrant and hopeful would our lives become? We would find ourselves cherishing the moments that once seemed mundane and finding strength in the trials that once seemed insurmountable. Our hearts would be lighter, and our spirits more resilient.

The simple act of changing our perspective can have a profound impact on our daily lives. It encourages us to be more grateful, more patient, and more compassionate with ourselves and others. It fosters a sense of wonder and curiosity, inviting us to explore the world with open hearts and minds.

So, as you go through life, remember to look for the wishes among the weeds. Celebrate the small victories, find joy in the unexpected, and allow yourself to be surprised by the beauty that surrounds you. Let each dandelion you encounter remind you of the endless possibilities that life has to offer.

In the end, it is not the challenges we face that define us, but how we choose to respond to them. By seeing the world through the lens of hope and possibility, we can turn even the most daunting obstacles into opportunities for growth and transformation. Embrace the wishes, let them guide you, and watch as your life blossoms in ways you never imagined.

I Am a Breathtaking Hot Mess

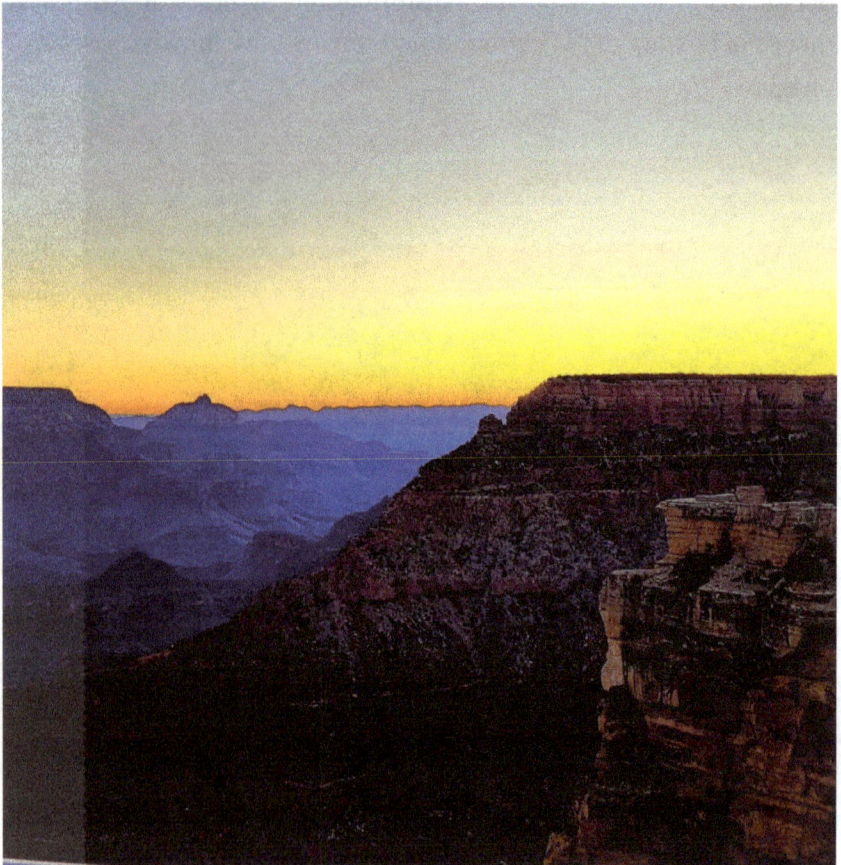

I Am a Breathtaking Hot Mess!

Yesterday was my 44th birthday. I stood before the Grand Canyon with my kids, seeing it for the first time. It was breathtaking. I learned that the devil keeps taking things away and trying to leave this hole in my life. It sometimes feels like a cut the size of the Grand Canyon, but even when there is a giant void, and this was not what I planned, It has still turned into something beautiful.

As we came through the park gate, I shared Our story with the park ranger. She cried and said you have no idea how much I needed to hear this today! Just think if someone had decided that the canyon was a mess not worth seeing. I am a breathtaking hot mess and have many stories for God.

I have decided to write them down to share how God shows up in my life with the world. Sometimes, we know exactly what we need to do, but we are afraid to do it! Because what will everyone think? What if God doesn't use this for good, and people turn away because I left my abusive husband? What if they can't understand why I keep believing after so many heartbreaks and losses?

I realized yesterday that some things can't be understood from the beginning or even the middle. They can seem catastrophic, like a flood or the washing away of a lot you thought you needed to survive! But then you climb out of the valley like a canyon floor, catch your breath, and look around. You realize how beautiful your life is even though it is still challenging, and you still have a race to run.

I am not even halfway through this road trip. And like my hot mess life, Some parts have been complex, but I absolutely would not change them for the lessons learned, the memories made, and the way I have seen God show up.

I have also learned to embrace the unpredictability, the twists, and the turns that come along the way. It's in those unexpected moments that we often find the most profound lessons and the deepest joys. My journey is far from perfect, but it's mine, and it's filled with the grace and guidance that I trust will lead me exactly where I need to be.

As we stood there, gazing at the vast expanse of the Grand Canyon, I felt a surge of gratitude. I am grateful for my children, who have been my constant companions and sources of strength, and for the resilience that keeps me moving forward. I found myself silently thanking every challenge, every setback, and every heartbreak that has shaped me into the person I am today.

This birthday, standing on the edge of something so magnificent and ancient, I made a promise to myself. I promised to continue to be vulnerable and open, to share my story in the hopes that it might inspire someone else on their journey. I promised to celebrate the beauty in the brokenness and to trust that every void can be filled with something wonderful, even if it's not what I originally envisioned.

Life is a series of breathtaking vistas and daunting valleys, and I'm learning to appreciate both. As we left the Grand Canyon, I felt a renewed sense of purpose and peace, knowing that every step of this journey is leading me to a place of greater understanding and deeper faith. Here's to the road ahead, with all its uncertainties and surprises, and to the unwavering belief that, in the end, it will all make sense.

Nowhere To Turn Around

Nowhere To Turn Around.

During our recent trip to the Great Smoky Mountains, I enjoyed incorporating valuable lessons into our adventure for my homeschooled children. We visited some historic battle sites and were pleasantly surprised to discover that God had some lessons He also wanted to incorporate. As someone who fears the uncertainty of the future, this experience reminded me of the importance of embracing the unknown and finding beauty in unexpected moments.

Have you ever been in the mountains and found that Google Maps is only sometimes reliable? It often reroutes you mid-journey and leaves you far from your intended destination. This is why we have learned to carry what my children refer to as a pirate map (atlas)! As we turned off the interstate, I assumed we would find an easy-to-reach paved spot with plaques to read and learn. I was half right.

We turned onto a smaller two-lane highway, which was slower but still drivable. That road soon turned into a smaller two-lane road with no defining markings for the center, even slower but still okay. Eventually, the road turned into gravel, which was not what I had planned. I considered turning around, but my kids were excited about standing in a place they had only read about in history books, so I turned onto the gravel road. As the road got narrower and less traveled, my anxiety level climbed. I was on the road, there was nowhere to turn around, and I stopped to pray.

That's when I realized this adventure was a lot like my life! I was already doing the thing I was afraid to do, and the thing I wanted most was just on the other side of that fear. Sometimes, turning around is not an option. Your only job is to move forward in faith, even if you can't see where this "road" is taking you, even when it turns into something that looks a little scary. And especially when you feel like stopping, pray and keep moving.

It is okay to be afraid. Courage is being afraid and doing it anyway. When we arrived at the paved parking lot of the battle site, I was relieved to see real restrooms and a gorgeous pavilion adorned with plaques to read. Isaiah ran to the cannon and proclaimed that this was the best history lesson he had ever had!

As we explored the battle site, the kids' enthusiasm was contagious. They eagerly soaked up every bit of information, their eyes wide with wonder as they imagined the past coming to life around them. We walked through the trails, reading about the bravery and sacrifices of those who had fought there. It was a humbling experience, a reminder of the resilience and strength that resides in all of us.

In the quiet moments between the kids' excited chatter, I found myself reflecting on the journey that had brought us here. The twists and turns, the moments of doubt and fear, and the ultimate joy of discovering something beautiful and meaningful. It was a testament to the idea that sometimes the most rewarding experiences are the ones that challenge us the most.

As the sun began to set, casting a golden glow over the mountains, we gathered around a picnic table to share a meal. Laughter filled the air as we recounted the day's adventures, and I felt a deep sense of gratitude for this time with my family. The mountains, with their wild beauty and hidden lessons, had given us more than just a history lesson —they had given us memories that would last a lifetime.

As we packed up to leave, I took one last look at the breathtaking scenery. The mountains stood tall and unwavering, a symbol of the strength and courage we all hold within us. I knew that, just like the road we had traveled, our journey was far from over. There would be more challenges to face, more fears to conquer, and more unexpected beauty to discover.

And so, with hearts full and spirits lifted, we made our way back down the gravel road, ready to embrace whatever adventures lay ahead. The Great Smoky Mountains taught us that sometimes the best way to navigate life's uncertainties is to trust in the journey, have faith in ourselves, and always be open to the lessons that come our way.

Today, I encourage you to take that leap of faith and trust that the road will lead you where you need to be.

The Power of Faith in Friendship

The Power of Faith in Friendship.

I can't count the times I didn't see a way, but my friends were like, "We are going to pray and trust that it will work out just as it should."Jesus saw their faith. When you surround yourself with people who have faith in the unseen, miracles happen! Find friends willing to not only carry you to Jesus but friends who are simply crazy enough to have the kind of faith to dig a hole in the roof and lower you down!

Having a strong support system is crucial in times of difficulty. It is easy to get bogged down by the weight of our problems, and it can be hard to see a way out. However, when we surround ourselves with friends who have faith in the unseen, we open ourselves up to the possibility of miracles.

Jesus recognized the faith of the friends who dug a hole in the roof to lower their paralyzed friend. Their unwavering belief that Jesus could heal their friend was what made the miracle possible.

In my own life, I may not need to dig literal holes in the roof, but I can still benefit from the kind of faith that those friends had. Finding people who are willing to pray for us and trust that everything will work out can make all the difference in the world. So, I choose to seek out friends who will carry me to Jesus and who will stand with me in faith when I cannot see the way forward.

Together, we can create an environment where faith thrives and miracles become a part of our daily lives. It is in these moments of collective belief and support that we find the strength to overcome our challenges. When we feel weak, our friends' faith can bolster our own, reminding us that we are never truly alone.

Let's strive to be those friends as well—those who offer unwavering support and encouragement. By doing so, we not only uplift others but also cultivate a community where hope and faith are abundant.

Remember, it's not just about receiving help; it's about giving it freely and with a loving heart.

In essence, the power of faith, collective prayer, and mutual support can transform even the most daunting situations. So, let us cherish our friendships, nurture our faith, and always be ready to dig metaphorical holes in the roof for each other, paving the way for miracles to unfold.

Chaos and Grace

Embracing Chaos and Grace.

God is a God of hot messes. One thing I can relate to and that gives me a little peace is the grace that shows up in the bible. Jesus comes for all of it! You just must let go and trust. Are you willing to give it to Jesus when His way is chaotic? Sometimes, our response is like that in

Matthew 8:34. Not only are they afraid of him and his power, but he cost someone 2,000 pigs. Sometimes, his help is chaotic, and we don't see the whole picture. But when we learn to trust him more, we see life is better if He is in our boat.

Life can be very chaotic and messy sometimes, and it's easy to feel overwhelmed and lost. However, we can find comfort in knowing God is a God of hot messes. He is always present, ready to offer His grace and love no matter the situation's difficulty. When we surrender our worries and fears to Him, we can trust He will guide us through the storm.

Matthew 8:34 shows how Jesus' help can seem disruptive and costly. But we must remember that His ways are higher than ours, and sometimes, we may not see the bigger picture. It's important to trust Him even when we don't understand His methods. As we learn to rely on Him more, we will see that life is always better when He is with us. So let go of your fears and doubts, and allow Jesus to be your anchor in the midst of chaos.

Remembering that we are not alone in our struggles is essential. We have a community of people who love and support us and are willing to lend a helping hand. We should never be afraid to reach out to others and ask for help when needed. Together, we can weather any storm and come out stronger on the other side.

Additionally, we should try to find moments of peace and stillness amidst the chaos. Whether through prayer, meditation, or simply taking a few deep breaths, we can find moments of calm that will help us navigate through the messiness of life. Remember, it's not about having a perfect life but rather finding joy and gratitude amid imperfection.

In conclusion, life can be messy and chaotic, but we can find comfort in knowing that we are not alone. By relying on God, reaching out to our community, and finding moments of peace, we can navigate even the most difficult situations. So hold on to hope, have faith, and trust that there is always a light at the end of the tunnel.

A Journey of Faith and Uncertainty

A Journey of Faith and Uncertainty.

At the beginning of my spiritual journey as a Christian, I was taught never to pray for patience, as God would not grant that request. Instead, He would offer me opportunities to develop patience. So when I asked Him for help with my faith and trust in Him, I was not prepared for the life of chaos and uncertainty that He so graciously bestowed upon me.

Despite finding comfort in Jesus, my journey did not become any less chaotic or uncertain; it simply provided me with more peace amid the storm. Although the storm still rages on, there are moments when the chaos subsides, and I take a breath to appreciate the uncovered blessings. Before long, another life-altering decision must be made, and the storm rages on.

But I have realized this is the beauty of my journey with Christ. Every struggle, every moment of doubt, and every decision is an opportunity for me to grow in my faith and strengthen my trust in Him. Through the chaos and uncertainty, I have learned to lean on Him more and rely less on my own understanding.

The support and guidance of my community have helped me navigate the ups and downs of my journey. Having a group of believers to pray with, share with, and learn from has been invaluable. I have also found solace in reading the Bible and other inspiring books as they provide me with the wisdom and encouragement I need to keep pushing forward.

My journey with Christ has not been easy, but it has been worth it. It has taught me the importance of perseverance, patience, and trust in God's plan. I am still learning and growing, but I am grateful for every step of the way.

Each lesson learned and every trial faced has shaped me into a more resilient and faithful person. I have come to understand that faith is not about having a trouble-free life but about finding peace and purpose amidst the turmoil. It is about knowing that, no matter what happens, God is with me, guiding me, and molding me into the person I am meant to become.

In the quiet moments of reflection, I have found a deeper connection with God. These moments of stillness and prayer reveal the gentle whispers of His love and the subtle nudges toward the path He has laid out for me. They remind me that even in the darkest times, I am never alone.

As I continue on this journey, I am mindful of the blessings that come with each new day. The laughter of friends, the warmth of family, the beauty of nature, a cup of coffee—all these are reminders of God's presence and His immeasurable love. Each day is a new opportunity to trust Him more, to serve others, and to share the hope and joy that faith brings.

I have also learned to be kinder to myself, I am a hot mess, but accepting that I am a work in progress. Perfection is not the goal; growth is. And with each step forward, no matter how small, I am moving closer to the person God intends me to be.

In sharing my journey, I hope to inspire others who may be facing their own storms. Know that it is okay to feel uncertain and to struggle; these are natural parts of the faith journey. Embrace them, learn from them, and let them strengthen your relationship with God. It is through these very challenges that we come to truly understand the depth of His love and the strength of our faith.

Navigating Challenges
with Grace

Peace is found in navigating challenges with grace.

Six years ago, the prospect of the two-and-a-half-hour journey to the children's hospital in St Louis traffic with my terminally ill son filled me with overwhelming anxiety and dread. I recall praying for peace during the drive, tightly gripping the wheel, and occasionally uttering expletives when other drivers nearly caused accidents.

After countless trips spanning six years, I can now proudly say that I can complete the trip to and from the hospital without any swearing. This change didn't come about because all obstacles disappeared or driving conditions in St. Louis improved. Rather, I realized that when I prayed for peace, the answer wasn't always what I expected. Instead of removing challenges, it seemed that God presented me with more opportunities to adjust my reactions.

As I navigate the now familiar route to the hospital, I notice the usual hustle and bustle of the morning traffic. Cars zip by, merging in and out of lanes, as if in a synchronized dance. Despite the chaos around me, a sense of calm washes over me, a stark contrast to the anxiety that once gripped me tightly during this journey.

The transformation in my response didn't happen overnight. It was a gradual shift, like the changing of seasons, each trip offering a chance for growth and self-discovery. I've come a long way from the days of white-knuckling the steering wheel and letting out frustrated sighs at every close call. Now, I approach the commute with a newfound perspective, one that focuses on patience, resilience, and gratitude.

Instead of viewing the traffic as an obstacle to my peace, I see it as an opportunity to practice mindfulness and grace under pressure. Every honk, every sudden lane change is a chance to choose my reaction, to respond with understanding. In these moments, I find solace in the realization that peace isn't about the absence of challenges but rather the way we navigate through them.

So, as I continue this journey, I do so with a heart full of gratitude for the lessons learned on the road and a newfound appreciation for the blessings that come in unexpected forms. And though the commute may remain unchanged, I find comfort in knowing that the true transformation lies within me.

So, you'll find me here, expressing gratitude for the blessings without requesting a traffic-free journey. Instead, I embrace each trip as an opportunity to further refine my ability to remain centered in the midst of chaos. These journeys have taught me the invaluable lesson that life's true beauty often lies in the moments of struggle and perseverance.

It's during these drives that I reflect on the precious time I have with my son, cherishing every smile, every laugh, and every moment of connection. The hospital visits, once a source of dread, have become a testament to our resilience and the deep bond we share. They remind me that every challenge we face together strengthens our relationship and our ability to find joy amidst adversity.

I've also come to appreciate the small acts of kindness from strangers on the road—a driver letting me merge in front of them, a friendly wave, or a simple smile from a fellow commuter. These gestures, though seemingly insignificant, reinforce my belief in the goodness of people and the power of compassion.

As I pull into the hospital parking lot, I take a moment to breathe deeply and center myself, ready to face whatever the day holds. The familiar faces of the hospital staff greet us with warmth and care, their dedication and empathy serving as a constant source of comfort. We are not alone in this journey; we are surrounded by a community of support and love.

And so, with each trip, I continue to learn and grow, finding strength in uncertainty and hope in the face of challenges. The road to the hospital may be long and unpredictable, but it is also a path of transformation, resilience, and unwavering love.

In this journey, I've discovered that true peace is not the absence of adversity but the ability to remain calm and centered within it. It is a lesson I will carry with me, not just on the road to the hospital, but in all aspects of life. And for that, I am profoundly grateful.

Embrace The Darkness

Embrace The Darkness

One of my greatest loves in life is the night sky. I feel that we, as humans, often take its splendor for granted. We only seem to acknowledge its beauty on clear nights or during rare lunar phases, when the stars are exceptionally bright and alluring or the moon's shape is particularly striking. However, we don't often appreciate the vast and seemingly endless space that lies between them.

To truly appreciate the grandeur of the night sky, we must embrace the cold and emptiness that looms above us. It's in the darkness that we witness the divine and majestic magnificence that it holds. It's a reminder that there is so much more in the universe than we can ever imagine, and it's humbling to think about the vastness of the cosmos.

During times of despair and hopelessness, I find solace in the beauty and wonder of the world around me. The night sky is a constant reminder to cherish and treasure the moments of light that illuminate my path, even in the dark times. It reminds me that there is always something to look forward to and that there is always a glimmer of hope amidst the darkness.

No matter how distant,, every star tells a story of perseverance and resilience. Each constellation is a map of human history, mythology, and imagination, connecting us to our ancestors who once gazed at the same sky with wonder and curiosity. The night sky is a canvas painted with the dreams and aspirations of countless generations, a testament to our enduring quest for knowledge and understanding.

As I stand beneath the celestial dome, I am reminded of the delicate balance that exists within the universe. The interplay between light and darkness, order and chaos, mirrors the complexities of our own lives. Just as the stars shine brightest against the backdrop of the night, so too do our moments of triumph and joy stand out against the challenges we face.

In embracing the darkness, we also embrace the unknown, the mysteries that lie beyond our reach. It is this pursuit of the unknown that drives innovation and discovery, pushing the boundaries of what we know and inspiring us to explore new frontiers. The night sky serves as a beacon, guiding us toward a future filled with endless possibilities.

So, let us not shy away from the darkness, but rather, let us find strength and inspiration in its depths. Let us marvel at the beauty of the cosmos and allow it to ignite our sense of wonder and curiosity. By doing so, we not only honor the legacy of those who came before us but also pave the way for future generations to dream even bigger and reach for the stars.

Dear God, I guess I got the laundry

Dear God, I guess I got the laundry if you can take care of everything else.

I know that when I don't know how something is going to work out God hears my pleas and understands my desire for help. In contrast, He may not take care of the laundry. He is always there to support me in ways I may not expect. My job is to keep the faith and trust that I have the strength to handle whatever comes my way as long as I stay connected to God.

When life's burdens feel heavy, it's easy to get caught up in the mundane tasks and forget that there is a higher power watching over us. By acknowledging that even the smallest concerns are seen and heard, we open ourselves up to receive guidance and blessings in unexpected ways. Just as we tend to our laundry to keep our clothes clean and fresh, we must tend to our spiritual connection to keep our hearts and minds clear.

With faith as our constant companion, we can face any challenges that come our way with courage and resilience. Trusting in the support and strength that comes from staying connected to God allows us to navigate life's twists and turns with grace and gratitude. So, as I fold the laundry and go about our daily routines, I remember to also fold in moments of prayer and reflection, knowing that I am never alone on this journey.

In those quiet moments, when the world seems overwhelming and the weight of responsibilities presses down, I find solace in the simple act of pausing to breathe and reconnect with the divine. Each task, no matter how trivial it may seem, becomes an opportunity to invite a sense of peace and purpose into my life.

As I sort through the mountains of clothes, made by my mini-humans, I am reminded of the need to sort through my thoughts and emotions, to discern what needs attention and what can be released. The rhythm of daily chores becomes a meditative practice, a chance to align my mind and spirit with the infinite wisdom and love that God offers.

In times of doubt or struggle, I remind myself that faith is not about having all the answers, but about trusting that the answers will come. It's about believing that I am supported and guided, even when the path ahead is unclear. By keeping my heart open and my spirit attuned to the divine, I find the strength to persevere and the courage to embrace whatever comes my way.

And so, with each folded shirt and paired sock, I fold in a little more faith, a little more patience, and a lot more love. I trust that by taking care of the small things with grace and gratitude, I am also taking care of the larger picture, guided by a power greater than myself.

Choose Joy

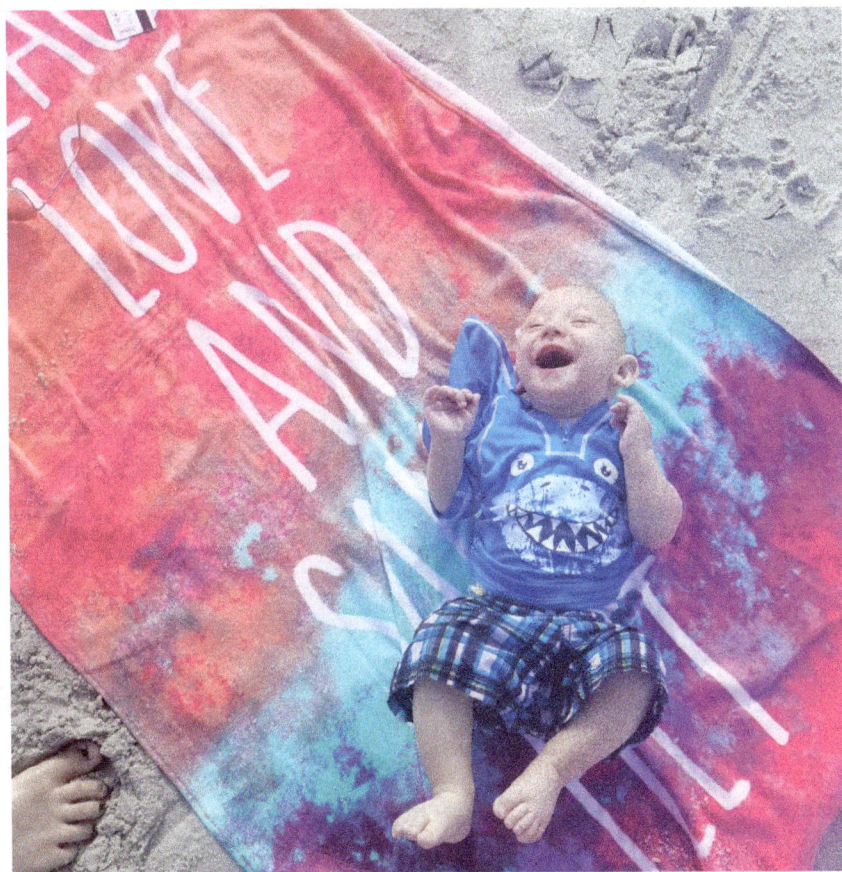

Choose Joy!

I was thrilled to become a momma again and all that goes along with parenthood. When my son, Elijah, was diagnosed with a rare terminal brain disorder Lissencephaly at six months, we were faced with a major decision: walk in grief and choose to be miserable like the world expected of us, or walk in faith and choose joy. And we chose joy. We chose to give him the best God-filled life possible!

I cannot imagine anything scarier than what I am currently facing with Elijah. Every day is a gift, he is the happiest person I know! For nearly six and a half years and counting, we have had this amazing guy in our lives! For the last six, we have known that our Elijah is dying amidst the sorrow we chose early on to love him fiercely and to live while he is with us here on earth. We made the decision to choose joy and living that out has come easily for the most part.

We have blogged about all our adventures as we work our way through Elijah's Bucket List, and many have commented on the fact that we are always smiling in pictures. This comment has always surprised me, and here is why…Elijah is here. Elijah is cognitively aware. Elijah is healthy. We have so much to be thankful for despite the constantly present, looming threat of death.

By making memories with him and sharing him with our family, friends, and the world we recognize there is a time to laugh, a time to dance, and a time to live. Death will likely come far too soon for this precious boy, and when that time comes, we will mourn and grieve. But not now. Joy is a daily choice for all of us, and it is one we make as a family each and every day. That choice helps us maintain our focus on enjoying him to the fullest. At the same time, the mix of emotions is difficult to describe.

Our adventures have been so fun and have filled our hearts with such joy. We have completed some items on his bucket list! We feel like a "normal" family doing "normal" things, and the diversions are refreshing. Yet, there are moments during our adventures when I am left speechless, overwhelmed with emotions. It is disheartening to realize that I shouldn't have to create a bucket list for my child, saddened by the thought of things he may never be able to do or experience.

One poignant instance was when my kids and I traveled to Florida to share his diagnosis with his siblings. The moment was filled with beauty, perfection, and joy, yet my heart ached to know my son would not witness such moments with his own children. I imagine us taking the trip again, his siblings relieving it with their kids, but he will never have that chance. Later that evening, as I expressed to Meagean how difficult it was for me to be there, she simply replied, "I know," understanding without words.

The joy and heartache coexist each day, vying for our full attention. Despite the heartbreaking reality, my heart swells with profound love and admiration when I see Elijah's radiant face and witness his happiness. He is perfect, beautiful, intelligent, and kind – a precious gift from God. He deserves our joy, love, and care. While the time for mourning may come, now is the time for joy, laughter, dancing, life, and love.

As we continue this journey with Elijah, we are reminded every day of the preciousness of life and the power of choosing joy in the face of adversity. Elijah has shown us the true meaning of resilience and love. Our days are filled with moments that we treasure, creating memories that will stay with us forever.

Despite the challenges we face, we are determined to live each day to the fullest, embracing every opportunity to show Elijah how much he is loved and cherished. His presence in our lives brings a light that shines brightly, illuminating our path with hope and gratitude.

We are grateful for the support and love we receive from our family, friends, and community as we navigate this difficult journey. Their kindness and understanding give us the strength to keep moving forward and savoring every moment we have with Elijah.

Together, we choose joy. We choose love. We choose to celebrate each day as a gift, embracing the beauty and wonder that surrounds us. And in doing so, we honor Elijah's spirit and the love that binds us all together.

Cleaning and Scrubbing

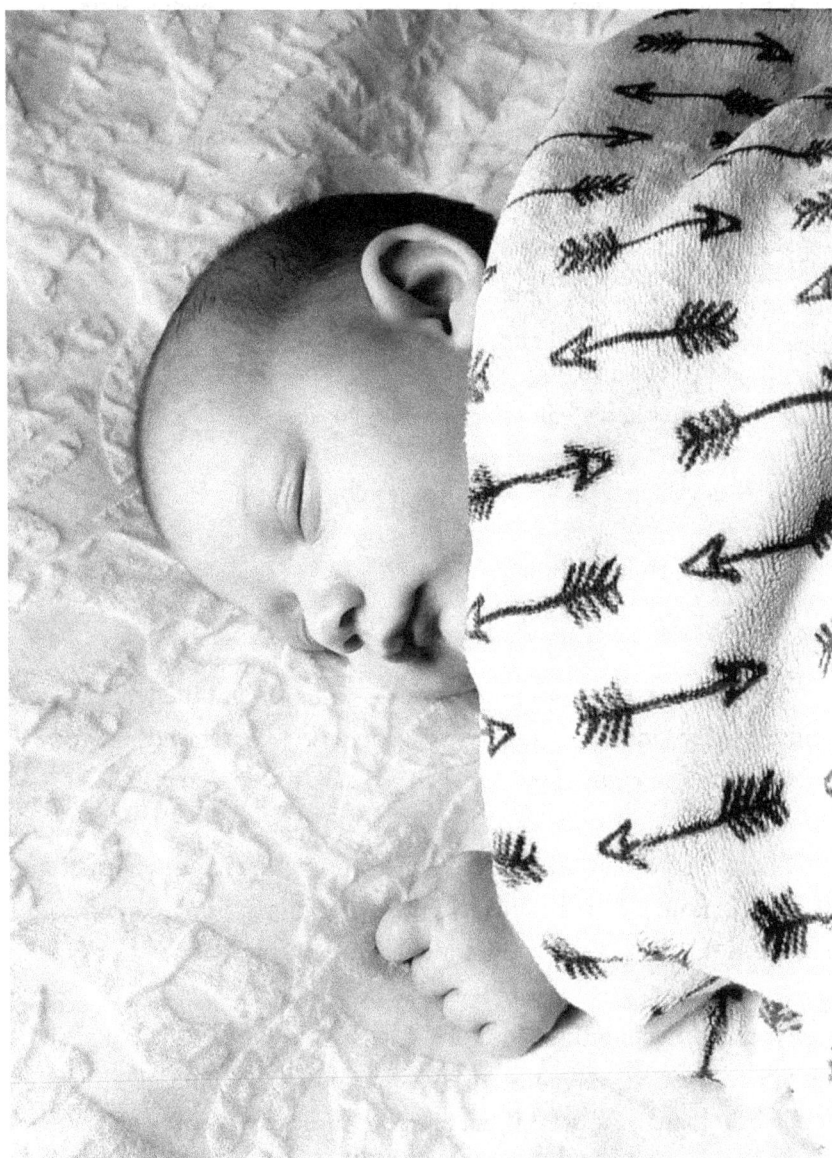

Cleaning and Scrubbing

Most days when they take a nap, I do the laundry because let's face it this laundry is never-ending, and I feel like I have people living here I do not know about. But today I chose to do less laundry and more life! Someday there will be no sleeping boy cuddles but laundry will be there. Remember "Cleaning and scrubbing can wait till tomorrow...babies don't keep."

Cleaning and scrubbing can wait til tomorrow

For babies grow up we learn to our sorrow
So quiet down cobwebs and dust go to sleep

I'm rocking my baby and babies do not keep.

-Ruth Hulburt Hamilton

This last verse is a song my mother and grandmother sang to me, and my older kids and I sang to my younger kids. It reminds me to soak up the time and enjoy them as much as I can.

Because solo parenting 5 kids one who is terminal is hard sometimes. I am up at 5:30 am. Just so I get some time with God and coffee before the crazy kicks in and I am pulled in 100 directions.

At times, despite this reminder, I struggle to find moments of tranquility to observe my children sleeping peacefully simply. However, when I do manage to steal these precious moments, I am overwhelmed with a sense of gratitude and love that fills my heart to the brim. It is in these silent moments that I realize how blessed I am to have these beautiful souls in my life, even if the challenges seem insurmountable at times.

I am reminded that amidst the chaos and demands of daily life, these are the moments that truly matter. These are the moments that make all the sacrifices worthwhile.

As I watch them sleep, I am filled with a sense of peace and content-ment. I am reminded that despite the hardships and struggles, there is love and a bond. So, as I cuddle him and kiss his forehead, I am grateful for these small, yet profound moments that remind me of the beauty of being their momma. Laundry not so much!

These are the moments that I will cherish forever, the memories that will warm my heart long after the children have grown.

So, I choose to embrace the chaos, find joy in the mess, and cel-ebrate the little victories each day brings. Whether it's a giggle-filled afternoon or a quiet bedtime story, these moments are the threads that weave the tapestry of our family life. And in this tapestry, every laugh, tear, and shared memory becomes a part of our unique, beautiful story.

As I navigate this journey of solo parenting, I remind myself that perfection is not the goal—presence is. Being present for my children, loving them fiercely, and showing them that they are seen and valued is what truly matters. The laundry can wait, but these fleeting moments of childhood cannot.

In the end, it is the love and laughter we share that will leave a lasting imprint on their hearts. So, I will continue to hold them close, sing them songs, and treasure every cuddle, knowing that these are the moments that define us as a family.

Am I the Problem

Am I the problem?

In Christianity, the phrase "come as you are" is commonly mentioned but not always practiced. How often do we judge those who appear different from us, whether it's a homeless person, a tattooed biker, or a frazzled parent with a lively child? By judging instead of showing genuine love to our neighbors, we unintentionally build barriers around the teachings of Jesus. This holier-than-thou attitude pushes away those we consider unworthy, contradicting His message of acceptance and love toward all. Jesus welcomed those burdened and weary, offering solace to those who sought Him.

Self-reflection, as highlighted in Romans 2:17–24, is essential to question whether we are part of the problem, especially when striving for self-righteousness and imposing high standards on others. This cycle of honor, shame, and pretense can isolate individuals from both religious and non-religious communities. We need to ask ourselves "Am I the problem? "

When we judge and fail to love our neighbors as ourselves, we inadvertently create a divide that distances people from the teachings of Jesus. It is crucial to break down the walls of judgment and self-righteousness and instead practice empathy, understanding, and genuine love towards everyone. By embodying the true essence of Christ's teachings, we can foster a community that welcomes all with open arms, embracing acceptance and love over judgment and exclusion.

By doing so, we not only honor the core principles of Christianity but also create an environment where everyone feels valued and respected. This transformation begins with small, intentional acts of kindness—offering a smile to a stranger, listening without judgment, and extending a helping hand to those in need. It is in these everyday moments that we can truly reflect the love and compassion that Jesus exemplified.

It's important to remember that everyone is on their own unique journey. Each person we encounter carries their own struggles, joys, and experiences. When we approach others with an open heart and mind, we allow space for genuine connections to form. These connections can bridge gaps, heal wounds, and build a stronger, more inclusive community.

In practical terms, we can start by engaging more deeply with our neighbors, volunteering our time, and being active participants in our local communities. Churches and religious groups can lead by example, creating programs that reach out to the marginalized and forgotten, ensuring that their doors are truly open to all.

Ultimately, living out the message of "come as you are" means embracing the diversity of humanity and recognizing that every person is made in the image of God. By setting aside our judgments and focusing on love and acceptance, we can create a world that mirrors the unconditional love that Jesus showed to all.

Surrender My Worries

Surrender my worries.

Trust in the Lord with all your heart. Sounds easy...I have been through some things in the last 15 years since I started walking with God. Dare I say things got harder after I did. But as I lay here in my quiet house listening to the birds in the Vinyard that is out my back door I am reminded that He takes care of them and me! He provides exactly what I need when I need it! In this season of my life, I am dealing with several health concerns for multiple kids and just recently received some of my own. But I know that the God who provided for that beautiful songbird is the same God who made sure that everyone had everything needed today! So today I will give it to God! And try to "Worry about today "as the scripture says.

Worrying about the future can be exhausting, so it's essential to focus on the present moment and trust that you are being guided on the right path. Like the songbird, share your unique melody with the world and trust that everything will fall into place. Embrace the strength and resilience within you, and know that you are not alone in facing life's challenges. Keep your faith close to your heart, and let it guide you through each day with hope and courage.

But if I am being honest, I will probably need to remind myself numerous times throughout the day that I gave it to him and that I do not need to worry about it. So today I pray that I can be more like the songbird who does not seem to be worried at all. Instead, she is sharing the song He gave her with the world! Although I am deeply grateful that, unlike the bird, I do not have to eat worms!

Remember to lean on your faith and trust that things will work out as they should. Life has a way of testing us, but it also has a way of revealing our inner strength and the depth of our faith. As you navigate these challenging times, hold on to the moments of serenity, like those spent listening to the birds outside your door. These moments are re-minders of the simple beauty and peace that exist even amidst chaos.

Take a deep breath and revel in the small victories and joys that each day brings. Whether it's a smile from a loved one, a kind word from a friend, or a moment of laughter, these are the gifts that help light your way. Allow yourself the grace to feel your emotions, but also the strength to rise above them.

Continue to share your journey and your songs with the world. Your story, your courage, and your unwavering faith can inspire others who might be walking a similar path. Remember, you are not just surviving—you are thriving in your own extraordinary way.

So, as you face each new day, let your faith be your anchor and your hope be your compass. Trust that the same God who cares for the songbirds is also watching over you and your loved ones, providing what you need at just the right time. Keep moving forward with grace, and know that every step you take is a testament to your resilience and faith.

Are We Truly Brave

Are we truly brave if we never encounter opportunities to be courageous?

God is ALWAYS teaching me lessons I have no desire to learn! At least not the hard way! Can't He just send me a really good book?! Yesterday I learned a lot about trusting God with them!

When we were visiting Orange Beach Alabama Avayha and Isaiah had the opportunity to go parasailing. It was a learning experience for me and them!

Somehow I feel like I can keep them safer than He can. Or they need me and Him.

It is easy to say I trust him with them when they are squabbling over who needs to load the dishwasher but when they were tethered to a speedboat hanging from a giant kite. This momma's faith was wavering ever so slightly. Who are we kidding I was terrified! While I tried not to show it. My heart left the boat with them.

As they ascended into the sky dangling from a kite. I felt an unexpected peace. Like God said, "I got this Amy!" Sometimes I forget he loves them more than I do.

God is good even when things seem scary. Although sometimes for me at least...it takes your children being tethered to a speedboat for you to learn more about God, faith, and trust!

Reflecting on courage, I ask: Are we truly brave if we never encounter opportunities to be courageous? Courage can mean soaring high in the air, but it can also mean relinquishing control and trusting in God.

He often imparts lessons in unexpected ways, even when we may be hesitant to embrace them.

Genuine courage isn't always about grand gestures but can also be found in surrendering and having faith in God's greater plan, even when it feels like we're soaring into the unknown. As the parasailing adventure came to an end and my children returned to the boat, their faces glowing with excitement and triumph, I realized that this experience was as much about my growth as theirs. They had faced their fears and soared above the ocean, and in doing so, they unknowingly helped me confront my own fears about letting go.

Back on the shore, their laughter was infectious, and I couldn't help but smile, feeling a newfound sense of gratitude. Gratitude for their safety, for the lessons learned, and for the reminder that faith is an ongoing journey. Watching them run along the sandy beach, I felt a deeper connection to the idea that true bravery often involves letting go and trusting in the unseen.

As the sun began to set, casting a golden glow over the horizon, I took a moment to reflect on the day's events. Life is full of moments that challenge us, push us out of our comfort zones, and test our faith. But it is in these moments that we grow, learn, and ultimately become stronger.

So, the next time you're faced with a situation that feels overwhelming or frightening, remember this: Sometimes, it takes being tethered to a speedboat or facing a daunting challenge to truly understand the depth of our courage and the strength of our faith. And in those moments, when you feel your heart pounding and your fears rising, take a deep breath and trust that you are never alone. God is always there, guiding you, loving you, and teaching you—sometimes in ways you least expect.

Your Inner Jar of Pickles

Embrace Your Inner Jar of Pickles: Finding Value in Others' Perspectives

As I wrote this book I must admit I had doubts. I doubted that I could actually write a book. I doubted so much. I had a friend write the foreword for me and when I read it I realized it made me uncomfortable. I am quick to notice ALL my own negative qualities. If she had simply said, "That Amy She's a HOT MESS!" I would have sipped my coffee from my oversized mug which can only be described as a bowl and nodded my head in agreement! But she can see all the things I can not see.

It's impossible to see yourself the way others see you; you can't view yourself from an external perspective. You're like a jar of pickles, only able to see the white backside of the label from your position. But to everyone else, you're visible in the jar, and to them, you might be an incredible jar of pickles, perhaps even their favorite.

They have the vantage point to appreciate aspects of you that you may never see. So, when someone expresses love and admiration for you, even if it's difficult to perceive from your standpoint, hold onto their words. Eventually, you may come to understand that everyone, including you, has value to offer, and you might just become someone's favorite jar of pickles. Remember, just because you can't see all your own qualities doesn't mean they aren't there.

Every interaction, every kind word, every moment of connection you share with others allows them to see the full picture of who you are. Trust in the reflections they offer back to you, and let their perspectives help you build a fuller understanding of yourself.

Embrace the idea that your unique combination of traits, experiences, and quirks makes you special. In a world full of different jars of pickles, each one has its own flavor, its own appeal. Celebrate your individuality, and recognize that what might seem ordinary to you can be extraordinary to someone else.

So, as you navigate through life, give yourself grace. Allow yourself to be open to the positive feedback and love from those around you.

Over time, you might just start to see glimpses of the incredible person they see—a person worthy of admiration, love, and respect. And in doing so, you can find greater confidence and joy in simply being yourself, knowing that you, too, bring something valuable and irreplaceable to the world.

Navigating through this journey of self-discovery and acceptance is an ongoing process. It's about learning to appreciate the small, seemingly insignificant bits of ourselves that others might cherish deeply. It's about recognizing that our imperfections make us human, relatable, and real. Just as a jar of pickles isn't perfect but still appreciated for its flavor and uniqueness, so too are we valued for our distinctiveness.

Building a stronger sense of self-worth doesn't happen overnight. It requires patience, self-compassion, and a willingness to see yourself through the eyes of those who care about you. Surround yourself with people who uplift you, who see the best in you, and who encourage you to see the best in yourself. Their perspectives can act as a mirror, reflecting back the beauty and strength that you might overlook.

Remember that everyone's journey is different. The qualities that make you feel out of place or inadequate might be the very traits that make you stand out in the best possible ways. Your journey, your struggles, and your triumphs are all part of what makes you uniquely you. Embrace them, learn from them, and let them guide you toward a deeper sense of self-acceptance.

In moments of doubt, remind yourself of the compliments and kind words you've received. Write them down if you need to, and revisit them when you're feeling low. Let these affirmations become the foundation of a more positive self-image. It's not about becoming someone else; it's about recognizing and embracing who you already are.

So, I am going to continue to sip my coffee from my oversized mug bowl, nod along to the chaos that sometimes surrounds me, and smile at the thought that I am, indeed, someone's favorite jar of pickles.

I hope this reminds you that your worth isn't measured by your ability to see it but by the impact you have on the lives of those around you. And that impact is something truly extraordinary.

Cleaning Shoes

Cleaning Shoes.

I wrote this two years ago...I am sure God is pretty frustrated with me sometimes. But my book comes out in a few weeks and my shoes are SUPER CLEAN!

You know when God nudges you to get in the boat. Well, he keeps nudging me. But I realized the other night that I am running from God. Not physically but ya'll instead of finishing my book I have been doing important things like cleaning my shoes... shoes I just told my pastor's wife I haven't worn in years and likely never will because I have reached an age where stilettos hurt my back!

But they are clean! And as I sat there cleaning shoes I likely will never wear again I noticed that my baseboards are not as clean as I would like. So I started thinking about cleaning them. When I asked myself "What are you doing? ". And it dawned on me! I, my friends, am running from God and what he has called me to do! Do I need to clean my shoes before I get in the boat!? Absolutely not!

After a much-needed coffee break with one of my dearest wise friends, I realized I was afraid to get in the boat! But it's okay to be afraid and do it anyway! Do it afraid because he has never asked me to get in the boat alone! What are you doing today to avoid the things you are being called to do? I am here to tell you, that you are in good company! Let's remember that taking that first step, even when we are afraid, is where true courage lies.

Together, we can support each other as we embark on this journey, knowing that we are not alone. Just like cleaning those shoes was a way for me to procrastinate, we all have our distractions. It's human nature to seek comfort in the familiar, even if it means avoiding the important work we are called to do.

But imagine the possibilities if we channel that energy into our true purpose! Think about the impact we can make when we face our fears head-on and embrace the path set before us. Let's hold each other accountable and encourage one another to take those steps, no matter how small they may seem.

Today, I challenge you to identify your own "cleaning shoes" moment. What are you doing to avoid your calling? And how can you pivot towards action? It doesn't have to be a grand gesture; even the smallest step forward is progress.

Let's be each other's anchor, reminding ourselves that it's okay to be scared, but it's not okay to let fear stop us. When we get in the boat together, we harness a collective strength that is unstoppable. So, let's lace up those metaphorical shoes, step away from the distractions, and set sail toward our destinies. Together, we can navigate any storm and reach the shores of our dreams.

Let's get in the boat together! Because we are braver together!

30,000

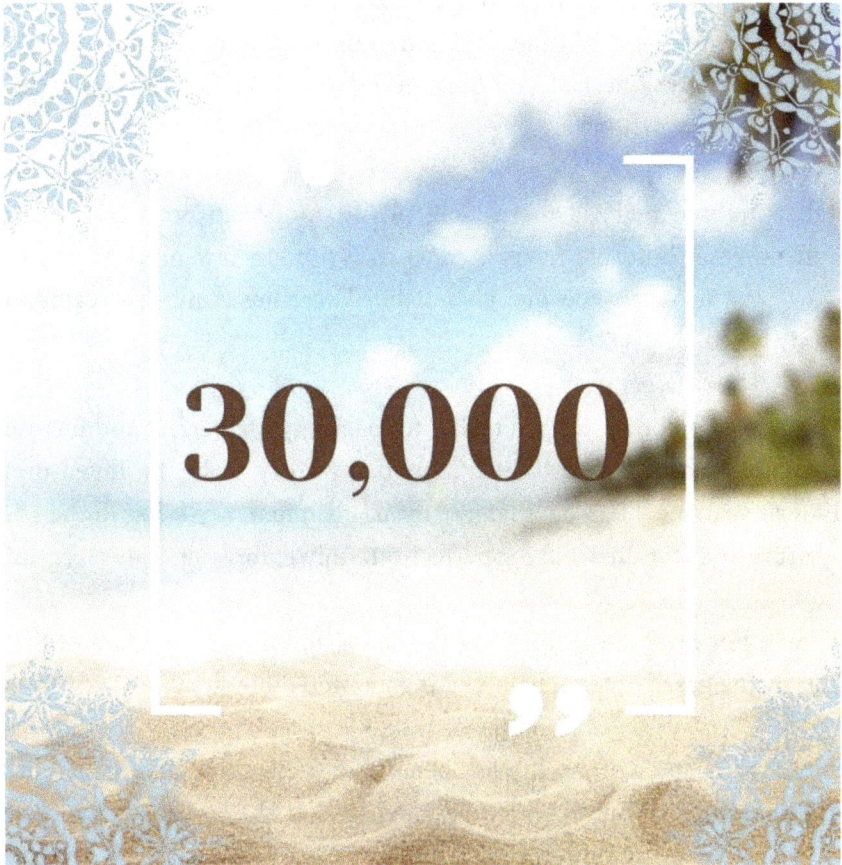

30,000

Embracing the chaos and unpredictability of
life!

I used to worry about all kinds of things, but I can remember the moment when I calmed down. I had just found out my husband had 3-5 years to live and one night, I couldn't sleep, so I was on my laptop. I read something online that said, "There are 30,000 days in your life."

At first, I didn't think much of it, but on a whim, I tabbed over to the calculator. I type in 34 times 365 and — oh my, I'm almost 12,410 days down. What the heck have I been doing? So that's how 30,000 ended up on the cheat sheet.

That night, I realized there were no warmups, no practice rounds, and no reset buttons. Every day we're writing a few more words of a story. And when you die, it's not like "here lies Amy," she came in 174th place."

So from then on, I stopped trying to make my life perfect and instead tried to make it interesting. I wanted my story to be an adventure! Eleven years or 4,035 days later, I think it's safe to say I found the adventure and lost the need for perfection, fully embracing imperfection!

I am a hot mess and embracing the chaos and unpredictability of life! But by the grace of God, I am writing an incredible story.

Every chapter of my life has been filled with surprises, challenges, and moments of pure joy. I've learned to cherish the little things and find beauty in the unexpected twists and turns. Whether it's spontaneous road trips, late-night conversations under the stars, or simply dancing in the kitchen, these moments have become the essence of my story.

I've also realized the importance of the people who journey alongside me. Friends who laugh with me, family who support me, and strangers who inspire me—all of them contribute to the tapestry of my life. Each interaction, no matter how brief, adds depth and color to my narrative.

As I look forward, I no longer fear the unknown. Instead, I welcome it with open arms, knowing that every new experience carries the potential for growth and discovery. Life may not always be predictable, but it is certainly an adventure worth embracing.

So here's to the chaos, the unpredictability, and the beautiful hot mess that is life. Here's to writing a story that is uniquely mine, filled with love, laughter, and endless possibilities.

The Quiet Heroes

The Quiet Heroes: Embracing the Power of Small Acts in Faith and Love

The Bible does not say a lot if anything about Mary's mother. She's just kind of a supporting background character. But recently one of my dearest friends lost her mother whom I also never met. My friend's name is Mary.

Which got me thinking.

I know that my friend's mother never thought of herself as special. Although her entire life she was doing small seemingly insignificant things for the kingdom. Teaching, guiding, and encouraging, those around her. Like a lighthouse. She likely never saw the size of the army she was raising for the lord this side of heaven. Although the people she sharpened have been walking alongside my family for years teaching, guiding, and encouraging us. I know that this family has touched thousands and thousands if not millions through a spark that a girl in the middle of Illinois started by having a little bit of faith and loving like Jesus.

I don't know if Mary's mother knew as she raised Mary and did all the little "just a girl in the middle of Jerusalem" things how important her work would be to the kingdom of God but today for me both of these incredible ladies remind me what can happen when I step out in faith and just continue to do the things I am called to do even if they might feel small and insignificant to me where I stand.

I am standing here folding laundry and reflecting on the countless ways that small acts of love and dedication can ripple outwards, touching lives in ways we may never fully understand. It's a humbling reminder that greatness often lies in the unseen, the everyday moments of care and compassion that build up over time.

As I fold each piece of clothing, I think of the many hands that have shaped my journey, the quiet heroes who have left an indelible mark on my heart. I am inspired to carry forward their legacy, to weave my own thread into the vast tapestry of kindness and faith that blankets our world.

In these simple tasks, I find a deep sense of purpose. It is in the ordinary that we often find the extraordinary, in the mundane that we discover the divine. So, I will continue to do what I can, where I am, trusting that every small act of love contributes to a greater story, one of hope, grace, and transformation.

And as I do, I pray that we all might recognize the power within us to make a difference, to be beacons of light in our own unique ways, and to remember that sometimes, the smallest gestures are the ones that change the world. Thank you Jewel for gifting my family and the world the Aeilts family. Your legacy is a testament to the profound impact of simple, heartfelt actions.

In this moment of reflection, I am reminded of the countless unsung heroes who, like Mary's mother and my friend's mother, have quietly shaped the world through their unwavering dedication and love. Their stories are woven into the fabric of our lives, giving us strength and inspiration to continue our own journeys.

Each day presents us with opportunities to make a difference, however small they may seem. It is in these moments that we have the power to touch hearts, to lift spirits, and to forge connections that transcend time and space. We may never fully grasp the extent of our influence, but we can trust that our efforts are not in vain. They are seeds planted in fertile soil, destined to bloom in ways we may never witness.

So, I will embrace the ordinary with renewed vigor, knowing that every act of kindness, every word of encouragement, every thank you note, and every gesture of love has the potential to create ripples that extend far beyond our immediate view. I will honor the legacy of those who came before me by living with intention, nurturing the relationships that sustain me, and striving to be a source of light in the lives of others.

As I continue this journey, I am filled with gratitude for the lessons imparted by these remarkable women. Their quiet strength and unwavering faith serve as a beacon, guiding me toward a life of purpose and meaning. May we all find the courage to step out in faith, embrace our unique callings, and recognize the extraordinary power of the seemingly small and insignificant.

In the end, it is the collective efforts of countless individuals, each contributing their own unique gifts and talents, that create a tapestry of hope and transformation. Let us celebrate and cherish these contributions, for they are the threads that bind us together in a shared story of love, resilience, and grace.

There's Beauty in
the Mess

There's beauty in the mess!

I don't always watch the sun rise and set from work. But this week I
have more than I would like to!

I would really rather be working from home and making memories with my mini-humans. Instead, I was working in a rainstorm over-thinking life! I was soaked and cold and it made me question how I got here. I am a hot mess sometimes!

I got out to deliver a package in a downpour! I nestled it safely in a garage and hurried back to my truck. While trying to avoid a large mud puddle I slipped and landed in the cold mud. It made me laugh and pulled me out of that "I'm just a girl in the middle of Illinois " mindset. I started to think a little differently. Especially after my Zoom Bible study from the car!

Our lives can feel, messy, unattractive, and dirty. We can feel like we're dodging one pothole after another, driving through one storm after another, and wondering if the rain will ever end. Playing out worst-case scenarios in our heads. But here's the thing about our worst-case scenarios, they are powerless against an all-powerful God.

God takes our hot mess and makes it a masterpiece!

The stuff you're stressed out about?
    God can replace your stress with a heart full of humility and His beautiful grace.

The regret and failures you're holding onto?
    God can take those experiences and teach you wisdom.

The pain that cuts you to your core?
    God can use that to draw you closer and closer to Him.

You are never too messy for God!

The truth is, this one beautiful life we get to live is really messy. So often we trip over our hopes and desires, only to fall into the messes we've been avoiding all along. What I'm discovering is when we fall into the very mess we hoped to avoid, we often find God's goodness there.

The things in your life that feel the messiest, the most broken, the ugliest are the exact things God will use to mold you into exactly who He intended you to be.

It's what makes you, YOU. It's part of the tapestry of experiences that makes you a work of art. If you're feeling like your life is too messy right now, if you're overwhelmed with regret, if you feel like a hot mess I encourage you, to take a good, long look at the pictures in this book. See how beautiful the day can be. Marvel at what God created and remember what God can do with your messy life. Remain in His hands, and let Him transform you into His masterpiece.

And remember, there's beauty in the mess. There's beauty in the mess, indeed. Each stumble, each fall, each moment of doubt and fear is a brushstroke in the grand painting of your life. It's through these imperfections that we can truly appreciate the fullness of our journey. Embrace the rain, the mud, and the unexpected detours, for they are shaping you into a person of depth and resilience.

As you navigate through the storms of life, remember that you're never alone. There is a profound strength in vulnerability and an exquisite grace in surrendering to the process. Your story, with all its twists and turns, is uniquely yours and holds the power to inspire and uplift others.

So, the next time you find yourself caught in a downpour, remember to laugh. Let it remind you that even in the darkest moments, there is light to be found. Let it remind you that every mess has the potential to become a message, every test a testimony.

Keep moving forward with faith, and let your heart be open to the countless ways in which life's messiness can reveal profound beauty. Your journey is a testament to the incredible transformation that is possible when we trust in something greater than ourselves.

In the end, it's not about avoiding the mess, but about finding the beauty within it.

We are Baver Together

We are braver together!

When my dear friend LuAnn Kleemeyer left for "someplace warmer " she gave me this picture of a coffee cup.

It hangs above my desk reminding me that God sends people and that I am not doing this alone! We are braver together!

So Find your tribe! You know the ones that make you feel the most YOU! The ones who lift you up and help you remember who you really are! The ones that remind you that a bump in the road is just that, a bump. And

" If this is the worst thing that happens today, it is still a good day." -LuAnn Kleemeyer

When you walk out of a room or end a Zoom meeting, they are the ones that make you feel like a better person than when you walked in. They are the ones that even if you don't see them face to face as often as you like, you see them heart to heart!

You can share your life, even the hard stuff, and they pray you through it! They stand or sometimes sit beside you in the dark. Sometimes crying too! Because some things can't be fixed only carried, you need a good friend who will send you tissues because she knows you will need them in this season!

Fierce friendships where you aggressively believe in each other, defend each other, and think the other deserves the world! No competition, no judgment. Just God's love pouring out on you through them. My cup is full, and my tribe is sent from God! Who's your tribe?

Finding your tribe is more than just having friends; it's about creating a community that feels like home, where love and support are unconditional. When life gets overwhelming, these are the people who remind you of your strength and worth. They see the best in you, even when you struggle to see it yourself.

Your tribe is there to celebrate your victories, no matter how small, and to hold your hand through the challenges that seem insurmountable. They are the ones who text you spontaneously, just to check in, and who remember the important dates and milestones in your life. They cheer for your dreams and stand by you when you face your fears.

In a world that often feels disconnected, finding your tribe is like discovering a hidden treasure. It's a bond that transcends distance and time, a connection that feels timeless and unbreakable. These relationships are not just about shared interests but shared souls, where you can be your most authentic self without fear of judgment.

So, cherish your tribe and nurture those connections. Be the friend who listens, supports, and loves unconditionally. Because in the end, it's these relationships that truly enrich our lives and fill our hearts with joy.

Photo credit LuAnn Kleemeyer from someplace MUCH warmer!

Divinely Directed Detours

Divinely directed detours.

One time in a small group Bible study a very wise man said "You can't really preach until you have buried your mother." I felt that! Chuck Sackett has always had a way of speaking directly to my soul.

Today was my mom's birthday. And oh how we celebrated! More than 13 years after her death, what she taught me still resonates! My mother wasn't perfect, but in her imperfect humanness, she was an amazing fountain of wisdom. That opened the door to my relationship with Christ, changed my life, taught me that God sends people, and gave me the faith I have today!

Sometimes our life looks nothing like we imagined it. Because we lack the imagination to see what can happen when we take a Divinely directed detour. Just one example of the many things that she taught me!

Sometimes life is not fair, and we can suddenly find ourselves facing circumstances out of our control. But we are never alone! My mom lived for 50 years. Amid the difficult circumstances of life, when things don't go as we planned we still get to choose how we will respond.

We can find comfort in knowing we are not alone. Did you know that at one point even Jesus could no longer stand and carry the cross and that's when Simon of Cyrene comes into the story? The Bible does not give us much information about him. But I wonder how he got there. What brought him to that place?

It must have been humiliating to walk through the streets with those criminals, Simon did not have a choice he had to do it. Sometimes life is not fair, and we can find ourselves facing circumstances out of our control. During those circumstances, the only thing we control is how we will respond.

I believe God sends people so we can find comfort in knowing we are not alone. I believe Simon chose to carry the Cross with compassion and in the end would develop a relationship with Christ that would change his life. And that's exactly how it works for us! When we find ourselves in a position we can not fix what do we do?

Life is hard and unfair at times, but we all get to choose how we will live within that framework and I believe that God strengthens us in the difficult times. The last five years have taught me that some things in life are not meant to be fixed only carried.

But with the support of others, the weight of these things can seem a lot less heavy! I know personally, that there are things in my life I cannot carry alone! I thank God every day for sending me people who help me carry them when I do not feel like I can.

Today was an extra special day and I am forever grateful for Divinely directed detours and the people God has placed in our lives who make the hard days a little easier!

We often underestimate the power of community and the strength that can be found in the bonds we share with others. Just as Simon of Cyrene stepped in to help Jesus bear the weight of the cross, we too can lean on those around us during our most challenging times. It's a reminder that we are never truly alone, even when the path ahead seems insurmountable.

As I reflect on my mother's legacy, I realize that one of her greatest gifts to me was the understanding that faith and resilience go hand in hand. She taught me that life's trials are not meant to break us but to build us up, shaping us into stronger, more compassionate individuals. Her wisdom continues to guide me, particularly in moments when I feel overwhelmed by life's burdens.

Today, as we honored her memory, I felt a deep sense of gratitude not only for her teachings but also for the people who have walked alongside me on this journey. These Divinely orchestrated connections have been a source of immense comfort and strength. They remind me that, like Simon, we all have the capacity to be bearers of support and hope for one another.

In celebrating my mother, I am reminded of the importance of celebrating the people in our lives who lift us up. Their presence is a testament to the love and care that God places in our path, ensuring we never have to face our struggles alone. It's in this communal support that we find the courage to persevere, embrace life's detours, and continue moving forward with faith and hope.

So, on this special day, I choose to honor not only my mother's memory but also the incredible network of support that surrounds me. I am thankful for each person who has been a beacon of light in my life, helping to carry the weight of my burdens and making the journey a little bit easier. Together, we can face life's challenges with grace and resilience, knowing that we are never truly alone.

Run That Race

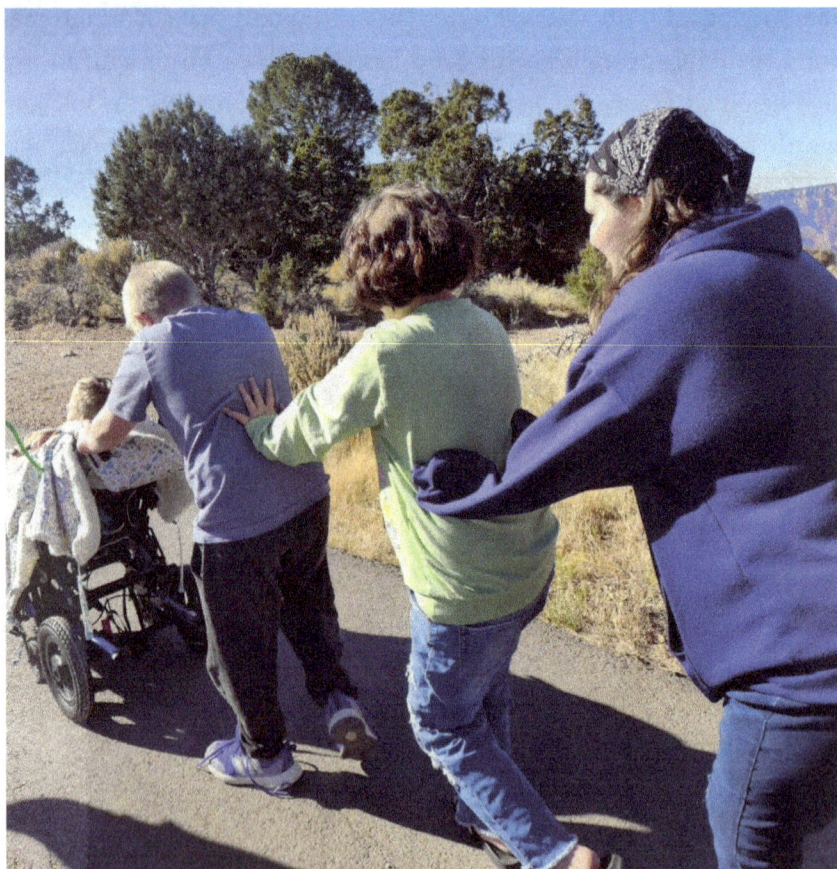

Run that race that has been placed before you.

As I wrote this book and continue on this journey I am reminded that we are all here for a reason. As much as I would like someone else to do some of the hard parts for me I am reminded, You have to run your own race. No one can run it for you. They can show up, run alongside you, push you, carry you. Sit with you when you fall. Hand you water and send you signs of encouragement. Cheer for you. Give you running shoes. But in the end, you are in charge of finishing you must keep moving forward even when you do not think you can.

Sometimes life's challenges may seem like a marathon, tempting me to alter my course when faced with difficulty or dissatisfaction. Instead, I am learning to pay attention to the signs and wisdom shared by those God has placed in my path, guiding, and encouraging me along the journey.

Picture being halfway through a triathlon and suddenly deciding the biking part stinks and I am going to switch to a motorcycle Instead, we must embrace the challenges that come our way and push through them with determination and perseverance. Each obstacle we face is an opportunity for growth and self-discovery. Just like in a marathon, the journey may be long and arduous, but the sense of accomplishment and pride we feel at the finish line makes it all worth it. So, keep running your race with courage and faith, knowing that every step brings you closer to the victory that awaits you at the end.

Remember, the race you are running is uniquely yours. No one else can run it for you. Along the way, people may come into your life to support you - running alongside you, giving you strength, and offering encouragement. They can be your cheerleaders, providing you with the tools you need to keep going. However, ultimately, the responsibility falls on you to keep moving forward. Embrace your journey, stay true to yourself, and trust that you have the strength within you to reach the finish line.

Just like a marathon runner, you have the power within you to keep going, to push through the challenges, and reach your goals. The journey may be tough at times, but with each stride forward, you are getting closer to your dreams. Embrace the journey, celebrate your progress, and trust in your ability to conquer any obstacles that come your way.

So, lace up your shoes, take a deep breath, and keep moving forward with courage and determination. The finish line may seem far, but with each step you take, you are one step closer to achieving greatness. Believe in yourself, believe in your strength, and know that you have everything it takes to cross that finish line triumphantly. Keep going, keep believing, and keep shining bright on your incredible journey.

In the end, it's your determination and perseverance that will see you through. Every step you take, every hurdle you overcome, is a testament to your strength and willpower. Remember, progress is progress, no matter how small. So, keep putting one foot in front of the other, keep that finish line in sight, and keep believing in yourself. I will be right here cheering you on! You got this!

We are braver together and stronger than we often realize. Each of us is running our own race, but we are never truly alone. The collective spirit of those who support us, who cheer us on from the sidelines, and who share their own stories of triumph and struggle, adds to our strength.

As you navigate your path, remember to take moments to reflect on how far you've come, to celebrate the milestones, both big and small, and to find joy in the journey itself. The race is not just about the finish line; it's about every experience, every lesson learned, and every connection made along the way.

And when the road seems particularly steep, when your legs feel heavy and your spirit is weary, take solace in knowing that your perseverance inspires others. Your courage to keep going, to face each challenge head-on, lights a path for those who may be struggling behind you.

So, let your heart be light, your spirit be resilient, and your mind be determined. You are capable of amazing things, and every step you take is a step towards the incredible destiny that awaits you.

Together, let's keep running, keep striving, and keep believing in the extraordinary power of faith and the human spirit. We are all in this race of life together, and with each other's support, there is nothing we cannot achieve. Keep shining, keep pushing forward, and know that you are never alone on this journey. The finish line is within reach, and the victory will be all the sweeter for the effort you have put in.

Run with joy, run with hope, and run with the unwavering belief that you are capable of greatness. The world is watching, cheering, and believing in you every step of the way. Let's make every step count. We are Braver Together!

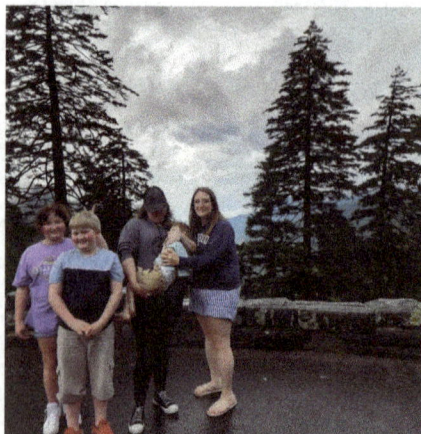

Amy Tarpein's narrative as a single mother raising ten children, including one with Lissencephaly, exemplifies bravery and resilience. In her book "Braver Together," she candidly recounts her experiences, blending challenges and joys while embarking on global escapades with her five younger children to create lasting memories and share their adventures with the world.

Renowned for her captivating storytelling and exquisite photography, Amy Tarpein is a highly regarded author. With a background in graphic design and creative writing, she expertly crafts tales that transport readers into her world and deeply resonate with them. Her writing spans various genres, such as blog posts, travel advice columns, and informative articles for prestigious organizations.

Amy's writing journey began in her youth, spending hours crafting stories and envisioning intricate worlds. This passion for storytelling blossomed over time, culminating in the publication of "Braver Together". Besides her Blog Elijah's Baby Bucket List, Amy has contributed to diverse literary magazines and anthologies, showcasing her versatility and writing prowess. She is a public speaker both in person and at global virtual gatherings, sharing her insights and experiences with others.

When not immersed in writing or caring for her children, Amy explores the world with her "mini-humans", delves into historical research while home-schooling, and treasures moments with her family. Her love for travel and adventure shines through in her narratives, infusing her work with authenticity and excitement.

Her commitment to community service is evident through her volunteer efforts with numerous non-profits, underscoring her deep dedication to giving back. Amy also nurtures a dream of establishing her own charitable organization in the future, driven by a desire to make a meaningful impact on the lives of others facing a terminal diagnosis.

Amy Tarpein continues to captivate and inspire readers worldwide with her distinctive voice and compelling storytelling, establishing herself as a beloved literary figure. Her journey serves as a testament to the resilience, love, and unwavering human spirit, motivating countless individuals to embrace their own narratives with courage and hope.

Elijah's story transcends mere bucket list accomplishments—it embodies embracing life with enduring joy and gratitude, irrespective of challenges. With his remarkable mother Amy and adventurous siblings by his side, Elijah traverses the globe, savoring every moment and demonstrating that life's beauty shines brightest in unexpected places.

Eager to partake in their heartwarming adventures? Follow their journey at elijahsbabybucketlist.com, where Amy chronicles their pursuit of joy and bold living. It's a tale that will inspire you to view the world through a lens of love, resilience, and boundless optimism.

Printed in the USA
CPSIA information can be obtained
at www.ICGtesting.com
CBHW071559110724
11466CB00005B/6